w/k 7

Complete
in
Christ

Dr Cameron fills a gap that has sometimes been widening among some Evangelicals in our generation. I have long believed that we need a rediscovery of Jesus' humanity, that we not only affirm that Jesus is God as though He were not man but that He is man as though He were not God. Many have not hesitated to affirm the former but are fearful to follow through with the implications of the latter. Dr Cameron is not so afraid, and his book is to be welcomed.

Dr. R. T. Kendall

I welcome this vigorously argued corrective to the other-worldliness that passes for piety in much evangelical Christianity–a salty dose of biblical commonsense about being human like Jesus.

David F. Wright

I warmly commend this clearly written book as an honest Christ-honouring and scripturally balanced work. I believe that an open-minded reading of it may well bring pastoral healing and perhaps personal liberation in various areas of the lives of not a few believers. One thing is for sure: it will hold your attention from the first page to the last.

Professor Douglas F. Kelly, Reformed Theological Seminary, Jackson, Mississippi, U.S.A.

Complete in Christ

Re-Discovering Jesus and ourselves

Nigel M. de S. Cameron

Marshall Pickering

Marshall Morgan and Scott
Marshall Pickering
Middlesex House, 34-42 Cleveland Street, London, W1P 5FB

British Library Cataloguing in Publication Data

Cameron, Nigel M. de S. (Nigel Malcolm de Segur), *1952-*
  Complete in Christ
  1. Man. Behaviour – Christian viewpoints
  I. Title
  261.5'5

  ISBN: 0 551 01715 5

Text Set in Plantin by Emset, London NW10 4EH
Printed and bound in Great Britain by
Anchor Press Ltd, Tiptree, Essex

Contents

For Lydia

Introduction:
Are Christians Human?

This seems a rather facetious question to ask. I ask it in order to draw attention to a striking omission in our thinking about the Christian life. For there are many influences at work in the church today which seem to imply that the right answer to it is *no*. Their idea of what it means to be a Christian requires us to rise above not simply sin, but human nature itself. The motive is commendable–to help us to be more spiritual. But it is a fundamental mistake to believe that spirituality lies in a denial of humanity.

The problem is that our human nature has been affected by sin, and we find it hard to imagine what it would be like to be human and yet sinless. Yet there is a human life which has been lived like that, and we must let the human life of Jesus govern our imagination and set the goals for our Christian living.

Above all else, if we believe in the fact of his humanity we must affirm our own. We must not be misled into thinking that there is any contradiction between being human and obeying God. Jesus has shown us what God made us for in the first place, and what in redemption he calls us to now: a human life that is obedient. This must be our goal, and we need to discern the subtle influence of temptations to deny that humanity in itself can be good.

The answer to our question *are Christians human?* is therefore an emphatic *yes*. The Christian life is the story of the renewal and affirmation of the image of God in us. In his son Jesus, God himself was not ashamed to become our brother man. Let us in our turn not be ashamed to be the men and the women he has called us to be in him.

Complete in Christ takes the following pattern. First, we set our thinking about the humanity of Jesus in the context of apologetics–the defence of the faith. Then we look at his humanity itself: what does it mean to say that Jesus was human? The focus then moves from his humanity to ours. We look in turn at four areas of human experience–the mind, the will, the heart and the flesh–and ask how our view of the Christian life should be affected by what we know about human nature. A chapter follows in which we turn to sin and its impact on our assessment of other Christians, and of ourselves. Finally, we come back to Jesus and the challenge of God's human face in him.

Some of the things that I say in this little book are likely to be controversial. I hope they are not also divisive. I have deliberately avoided naming people and books and movements to illustrate what I am saying, since the evangelical church is already too much divided. Where I have disagreed with views that are commonly held, I do so in deep respect for those who see things differently. I do not criticise in the disparaging spirit that is so easily destructive of our unity in Jesus Christ. We are called to speak the truth in love, and while this is not always easy, its twin obligations rest heavily on our shoulders.

So my aim is not to offend and divide, but to ask my brothers and sisters to look again at some of our cherished ideas and ask questions about them. In some of what I say I am speaking as much to myself as to anyone. My concern is not to come up with all the answers, and that is why–inevitably–the emphasis is on placing question-marks against some of our assumptions. Another and larger book would be needed to take the discussion forward into a balanced biblical assessment of the positive alternatives. It seems worthwhile, nevertheless, and at the risk of being misunderstood, to say what follows. My prayer is that it may encourage a fresh realism in our Christian living, and bring us back to the example of that most human of men, Jesus Christ, to whose image it is our highest calling to conform.

I am glad to acknowledge my thanks to the Faculty of Covenant Theological Seminary, St Louis, Missouri, who graciously invited me to give their Convocation address in 1986. I took as my subject, 'The Humanity of Jesus–then and now', and some key aspects of what I said on that occasion have given shape to the first two chapters of this book. I remain grateful for the stimulus which discussion there provided for my thinking, and retain happy memories of the gracious hospitality which was afforded me.

The argument which spans the chapters which follow was first developed in an address in Glasgow in 1987, under the auspices of Rutherford House.

Nigel M. de S. Cameron
Rutherford House, Edinburgh
7th March, 1988

CHAPTER ONE

The Challenge of the Incarnation

Christians today are in retreat. Whether this is a fair assessment of the church worldwide is another matter, but it is how we in the West see ourselves. We give special emphasis to the health of the cause of Christ in the ancient heartland that we call Christendom. This may be a mistake, and there is a growing realisation that the church's centre of gravity is moving elsewhere. But the idea that we are taking part in a retreat remains a true assessment of our psychological state. It is how we as Christians see ourselves.

Yet it is also more than that. Among the striking results of the decline of the church in the West has been the decline of the influence of Christian thinking in what continues to be the world's dominant culture. The areas in which the church was once strong continue to provide the intellectual leadership of much of the globe.

This collapse of influence has destroyed the self-confidence of the church. It has helped worsen the increasingly confused theological state of the mainstream churches. There is an almost desperate attempt to justify the church's message, and a readiness to adapt that message so that it will be more palatable to those who do not believe it. This inevitably involves a gradual process of bringing it into line with secular thinking.

The position of evangelicals is distinctive, though they have not escaped the general failure of morale which has given credence to all kinds of alternative theology. At the same time, they have faced a difficulty uniquely their own. With the fragmentation of the Protestant mind, they find themselves increasingly isolated from the contemporary mainstream of Christian tradition. They have found themselves cast in a new role as standard-bearers for the historic Christianity from which the mainstream of the church has departed. They are forced to defend distinctive and historic Christian beliefs that others in the churches have yielded; and in consequence they are engaged on two fronts—with an defence of the truth directed as much at mainstream theological opinion in the church as it is at the sceptic outside.

The Defence of the Faith

A striking feature of the modern evangelical movement is the emphasis on 'apologetics', the defence of the faith. Much of it is directed at questions which were not, historically, distinctly 'evangelical' concerns at all. It is a measure of the historic decline of the intellectual standing of conservative Christianity that its resources have come to be so largely employed in defending itself. Apologetics has taken the dominant place among evangelical intellectual concerns. This no doubt partly reflects the unease that Christians themselves feel when confronted by the intellectual challenge which is presented by the unbelieving mind of their generation. They constantly seek to reinforce their own convictions. Apologetics has always had spin-off benefits for believers, helping them think through the ground of their faith in the light of contemporary challenges, and preparing them for the personal apologetics in which—to some degree—they are all engaged. But in the modern evangelical church, matters have gone further. The consequences have been profound, and are to be uncovered in many other areas than those addressed in this book. For the first time since the Fathers of the ancient church, apologetics has come to assume major proportions today. This is to be expected, inasmuch as the mind of the West has finally ended its long affaire with the Christian faith. But for evangelicals the crisis has been peculiarly profound, since in major areas of belief, the mainstream church has seemed to join the sceptic in questioning historic convictions. So apologetics–*vis-a-vis* other Christians as as well as unbelievers–has taken on a new role.

Now this need be no bad thing, and it has certainly been necessary. But it has had side-effects, notably in its impact on the central area of the church's thinking: its dogmatics, its formulation and understanding of doctrine. For one thing, it has been simply overshadowed by the constantly growing importance of apologetics–in appeal and in apparent importance. Justifying the ways of God to man has taken over from expounding those ways, in every area of the life of the evangelical church: in the work of assemblies and synods, in pulpits and lecture rooms, and in writing and publishing.

The tendency in the church at large has been twofold: first to marginalise dogmatics as subordinate in importance because secondary to the apologetic needs of the hour; and secondly, to have the subtler effect of influencing the dogmatic agenda and its priorities in order to serve apologetic needs. Of course, it is natural that there should be interaction between these two departments of the church's intellectual life. But it is doubtful whether there has been sufficient awareness of the degree to which theological activity has come to be governed by apologetics.

This may seem abstruse, but its implications are both practical and profound. The tail has begun to wag the dog. The centre of gravity of our thinking about God has been shifted from true. The need to justify ourselves before a sceptical world has distorted our theological understanding. The piecemeal abandonment of the supernatural elements of the faith is the chief fruit of this process at its most destructive. Theologians, in the role of apologists–like rogue army commanders fighting a hopeless campaign–have taken upon themselves responsibility for the negotiation of an end to hostilities. They have tried to make peace with the secular mind by making one. What they have negotiated has been a credible Christian belief; but the idea of credibility with which they have worked has been secular.

To say that is to say the obvious. Less obvious has been the impact of this same tendency on evangelical orthodoxy. As has been pointed out, evangelicals have a special interest in apologetics, an apologetics directed partly–often chiefly–at the mainstream church; in defence of the historic faith which the church has come to doubt or disown–partly as a result of this engagement in nature might call apologetic by negotiation by mainstream theologians. Sometimes evangelicals have themselves follow the lead set by their colleagues. But at the same time (and partly in conscious reaction) there has been a contrasting effect. Undue weight has been given by evangelists to doctrine that happens to be controverted. Those things which have for some reason escaped the attention of the doubters have been neglected.

That apologetics should have come to play so important a part in the life of the evangelical church is perhaps inevitable. But it is undoubtedly a misfortune that it should so heavily influence the theological agenda of orthodoxy. It is not easy to quantify the price which has been paid, in the deleterious effects of apologetics on the theology which is supposed to be being defended. What is needed is an awareness of the silent distortions which constantly result from this process, if it is not checked. Since we can hardly lay less stress upon apologetics, we must consciously compensate for its distorting tendencies by deliberately giving more adequate emphasis to those areas of Christian belief which are not in the apologetic front line.

The Controversy about Jesus Christ

Nowhere is this more true than in our thinking about Jesus Christ. Here more than anywhere it is the currently controversial aspects of Christian belief that have engaged our interest, while the seemingly uncontroversial aspects have been ignored. The result has been a serious skewing of our Christian understanding, and it has had profound practical implications.

The central problem lies in the almost universal lack of interest, among evangelical Christians, in Jesus' human life and its significance. The fact that the Son of God has lived a human life amongst us is left high and dry. It is the message of Christmas, and the necessary prerequisite of the atonement; but it is little more. The story of the years in between, which occupies so substantial a part of the New Testament, is subject to serious and systematic neglect. The apologetic frame of reference in which so much theology is done–whether in the pulpit or the lecture room, or through the written word–has determined that there are other priorities.

So the divinity of Christ, with its attendant supernatural phenomena (the virgin birth, miracles, resurrection, and so on), since it has been everywhere in dispute, is a major focus of interest. His humanity, unsurprisingly, is not denied; and so it is passed by. In fact, the 'apologetics' in question is in practice largely the defence of the distinctive character of the conservative theological tradition. Arguments about the divinity and supernaturalness of Christ are largely held within the churches. It is these debates which have provided the context for the development of contemporary evangelical theology.

So the apologetic focus on the divine character of Christ has left his human nature in the dark. But we can go further. We can trace two separate though related paths by which this same result has been achieved. Alongside the direct implications of an emphatic apologetic concern with Jesus' divine nature, there is the equally pronounced interest in his death as over against his life.

Let us look first at this second strand. Evangelical theology has always focussed on the death of Jesus Christ, as the prime concern of the New Testament writers. Since the nineteenth century, there have been many attempts to portray Jesus in a new light–with interest in his life in place of his death, and partly in reaction to the atonement theology which dominates the New Testament. It is through such alternative theories that liberal theologies have found their rationale, whether (in extreme cases) seeing the death of Jesus as of no special significance at all or (more often) recognising its importance but focussing instead on aspects of his life.

As a result, there are two elements present in modern evangelical understanding of the significance of Jesus. There is the proper, biblical emphasis on the crowning importance of his death, as that to which his life looks forward even from its beginning. And there is an emphasis which derives from apologetics, seeking to redress the imbalance of liberal interpretations of Jesus. It too stresses the centrality of the cross, but does so in reaction; and in the process it downgrades the significance of his life. Whether directly or not, the importance of the human life of Jesus is underplayed.

Let there be no misunderstanding. The centrality in the New Testament of the message of the cross is undeniable, as is the fact that it should consequently have the dominant place in the teaching and preaching of the church. But if that dominance has the effect of excising other vital elements in our understanding of Jesus Christ, it is necessary that it be qualified. Our pattern of understanding must always reflect the pattern of the Scriptures themselves. And while the preaching of the cross is at the heart of the message of the New Testament, it is not all the New Testament has to say; or, to put it more carefully, the message of the cross cannot be isolated from its place in the warp and woof of its theological context in Scripture.

The point is well made by the use which evangelicals make of the New Testament itself. It is selective, in the sense that, in our teaching and preaching, we do not simply follow the weighting which is evident in the relative lengths of the New Testament books themselves. There are certain texts, chapters, and books which we see as having pivotal significance, and which accordingly have a special place in our thinking. It is on this ground that the letter to the Romans has rightly taken such a prominent place in the life of the church. What we must ask ourselves, however, is whether, in so stressing the significance of the death of Jesus, we are placing adequate emphasis also on the significance of his life.

We do not know why, in the providence of God, there are four gospels rather than one. Undoubtedly they are better vehicles for the multi-dimensional character of Jesus, which in a single book (like the many 'lives of Jesus' that have been written) would lose its depth and something of its objectivity. But we face the fact that there *are* four gospels, and that partly as a result, the story of the life of Jesus dominates the New Testament. Of course, the gospels climax in his death. But the fact remains that they offer us substantial testimony both to the fact of the incarnation and to the actual character of the human life which is led by the incarnate Son of God.

We possess no picture of the physical likeness of Jesus of Nazareth. To judge from the tenor of much modern evangelical Christianity, we no more possess an account of his life and his ministry. The interest is simply in the fact of incarnation and the divine nature of the incarnate one as premises necessary to the development of an understanding of his death. This might appear a caricature of evangelical thinking. It is certainly a caricature of the theology of the New Testament. There is much in the preaching and teaching of the evangelical church which belies such an image and better presents the gospel portrait of Jesus. Yet, even here, it is unusual for evangelicals to give considered and positive attention to the significance of the humanity of Jesus.

Which brings us back to the other strand in our argument. Evangelical emphasis on the death of Christ has led to the neglect of his life, partly in reaction against liberal theories in which the significance of his death is understated. An even greater neglect of the human life of Jesus and its significance has resulted from an absorption with the defence of his divinity.

Here the impact of apologetics has been even more marked. The principal thrust of liberal theology has been its attack on the divinity of Jesus Christ. This has rarely been direct, and actual denial of the incarnation remains unusual. But denials *in effect* have been common, as Christians have struggled to accommodate their beliefs to the standards of credibility maintained outside the church.

We have already referred to a kind of apologetics which is essentially concerned with 'credibility negotiation'. Its most powerful effect has been to divest much of Christian belief of its supernaturalism, its belief in points of contact between events in this world and forces in the world that is unseen. There is nothing more supernatural in the Christian faith than the incarnation itself, and it is around the incarnation that much of the supernatural content of the New Testament is to be found. Angels and the star announce his coming, Jesus performs signs and wonders, he claims supernatural knowledge and authority, rises from the dead and ascends bodily into heaven.

The irony of much of the debate about Jesus is that, while few have openly denied the central claim of incarnation–that Jesus was 'the Word made flesh'–there has been a general denial in the churches of some or all of the supernatural accompaniments of this central miracle. No doubt one reason for this is to be found in a hesitation to deny the central Christian doctrine. On the other hand, whether a miracle-story tells of something that actually took place, or whether Jesus' teaching was really reliable, can be presented as questions of historical interpretation. They seem to leave the doctrine of incarnation untouched, and trespass only upon the precise conditions under which it operated. Even something as seemingly fundamental as our Lord's bodily resurrection can be questioned without denying the central fact.

Whether in some such covert manner, or openly and directly,

a major theme of modern Christianity has been the denial of the incarnation as historically conceived. Whatever special qualities are believed to have attached to Jesus during his life in Palestine, a divine nature–understood as the church has always hitherto believed–has not been among them. So a major theme of evangelical apologetics has been the defence of the deity of Christ. Sometimes this has taken the form of a candid argument for incarnation, and its concomitant of a divine nature in Jesus; an argument offered to those who have equally candidly denied this doctrine. More often the apologetic thrust has focussed on lesser but related issues. The virgin birth and the resurrection, as the twin chief supernatural attestations of the incarnation; and the miraculous 'signs and wonders' which, according to the gospels, mark the public ministry of Jesus–all have been under threat, denied, and therefore all have been affirmed.

It is interesting to note the pattern of this argument. A good deal of energy has been put into denying the supernatural accompaniments of the incarnation, and to the evangelical this is in effect denying the incarnation itself. The New Testament picture is fragmented by such sceptical criticism. So in response, the evangelical asserts and underlines the credibility and the importance of these same supernatural accompaniments. That is to say, the more sceptical are his critics of the possibility of the supernatural in and around the ministry of Jesus, the more vehemently it is asserted.

Not only so. This kind of apologetic activity, which permeates serious and popular evangelical thinking alike, has had its effect on the sense of identity of those whose convictions it is intended to support and propagate. They come increasingly to see their beliefs–and their community–defined by the main lines of the argument offered on their behalf. So with this particular set of issues, evangelicals come to understand themselves as those who hold to these supernatural emphases in their beliefs about Jesus Christ.

The flashpoint of contemporary controversy becomes the focal point of theological understanding and identity. The believer and his community are affected in just the same way as the work of the theologian. Apologetics has become the dominant factor, and while there are wide differences, there is a curious parallel with the very different kind of apologetics in which the mainstream church has been engaged. There the aim (though unacknowledged and often unconscious) is credibility, so there is a constant process of adjustment of conviction so as to bring it closer into line with contemporary conventions of what is believable. Here–in evangelical apologetics–a converse but also parallel process is at work. What the canons of contemporary convention declare to be unbelievable is quietly evacuated by the liberal. By contrast, the evangelical strengthens the garrison. He asserts that which, in particular, is denied–denied as incredible in the world outside, denied as unnecessary, a stumbling-block to belief, by the liberal inside. Evangelical energies are directed to those points in Christian conviction which are perceived as most immediately vulnerable to sceptical assault.

So while liberal apologetics has the eventual effect of abandoning controverted beliefs, evangelical apologetics lays upon them special stress. The effect of this on doctrine has already been noted, and will be again: it tends to distort the balance of the historic faith. Its effect on the way in which the world outside perceives the Christian faith is also important, since in drawing increased attention to those points which are the most difficult to believe it distorts the way in which the faith is perceived. It tends to turn the Christian faith into a caricature of itself, in which the seemingly major elements (those which are most stressed) are by definition those which the unbeliever finds it most difficult to accept; and those which he could the more readily believe are neglected as of little importance.

Of course, apologetics also does more: when it is effective, it enhances or helps establish the credibility of those elements in the faith which the contemporary mind finds most difficult.

What needs to be recognised is that it can also be counter-productive; especially if its approach is to focus on particular, isolated points of contention.

Yet apologetics is essential, both as a formal discipline and as a necessary adjunct to the continuing preaching and teaching of the church. It is far from our intention to suggest that we can do without it. But as we recognise its distorting effect, both on what we believe and on how our beliefs are perceived from the outside, we are freed to take conscious action to correct the resulting imbalances. This is without doubt the case with the humanity of Jesus.

The Humanity of Jesus

The problem is that the necessary resistance with which liberal ideas of Jesus have been met by evangelicals has had the result, both in the evangelical mind and in the perception of the out-sider, of so stressing those 'supernatural' elements which in the New Testament accompany the narrative of the incarnation as to distort and disfigure the gospel portrait of the humanity of the incarnate Jesus.

As well as seeking to counter individual denials of the historic and supernatural character of the incarnation, the evangelical understanding of Jesus has been much influenced by the fact that a stress on his humanity has been a common feature of every mistaken contemporary understanding of him. There have been many attempted re-constructions of Jesus, in the image of their begetters. The simple liberal emphasis on the exemplary character of Jesus' life has gained wide currency, and it is pro-bably true to say that the common view of Jesus–outside the church and inside–is of a man whose life is intended to be an example to us; and nothing more. There have also been more distinctive models. The revolutionary idea remains popular, however plainly miscast the Jesus of the gospels may seem in the role of a zealot. More moderate versions see him as the champion of the poor.

To put it another way, every contemporary theology which has sought a distinctive social or political character has looked to the human life of Jesus (whether or not believing anything else about him) as its exemplar, and has sought to find in him justification for its particular purposes.

The effect of these uses of the humanity of Jesus has been to underline an evangelical lack of interest in the subject. In fact there have been two kinds of response to the development of social and political interest in Jesus' human life. Some evangelicals have been influenced positively, and have sought to introduce modifications into the more thorough-going interpretative schemes so as to bring Jesus' testimony, along with that of the Old Testament prophets, to bear upon social and political questions of today. Curiously, an interest in such a reading of the gospels has not tended to result in a renewed interest in the general question of our Lord's humanity. It has been an interest directed to particular ends. More commonly, of course, the effect has been to rouse evangelical suspicions. Since these characterisations of Jesus' humanity are generally the work of those who have little interest in his divinity, they are seen as dead-ends, demonstrations of the subjective and arid character of interpretations of Jesus which focus on his human life instead of his divine origins and his death.

Yet, although the humanity of Jesus may be the least contested of all Christian doctrines today, it is hardly the least significant. While he was no mere man, the Christian faith depends as surely on his being 'very man' as it does on his being 'very God'. The two ascriptions–which to the sceptic are, respectively, trivial and incredible–interlock inextricably in the mystery of the incarnation. There could be no incarnation without a Jesus who was divine, but it is no less necessary that Jesus was human. The Word was made *flesh*.

A powerful illustration of the neglect of this doctrine is to be found in one of the great nineteenth-century systematic theologies, though it is singled out simply to provide an example–there are plenty more. W.G.T. Shedd's *Dogmatic Theology* is in many ways an excellent work. But, like most evangelical theology, it is deeply influenced by the apologetic needs of the day. The work runs to three volumes, and includes a lengthy section on the deity of Christ, and a further lengthy discussion of the two natures (divine and human) and how they could subsist in the one person–a theological problem which has exercised the church down the centuries. But when we come to the chapter on the *humanity* of Christ, what do we find? Chapter 3 of volume II opens with the words, 'Christ's Humanity is undisputed'. Shedd briefly summarises the debates in the early church when it was in question. And then the chapter ends. It lasts less than four pages, and that not in a work on apologetics, but in dogmatic theology.

Now this is not an isolated case. It is an example of the manner in which the evangelical community has allowed its dogmatics to be governed by apologetic concerns. And it illustrates also the fact that an awareness of this tendency is the key to the redressing of the balance. Shedd could have written: 'Christ's Humanity is undisputed, but stands as a cardinal doctrine of the faith...' Moreover, his treatment of this 'undisputed' doctrine as if it were incidental to theological understanding suggests a common apologetic weakness among evangelicals. For there is a failure to exploit the fact that much of what we believe *is* 'undisputed'. Undisputed Christian doctrine provides a major meeting-point with the outsider, with its example of Christian belief that is in itself 'credible'.

Yet, partly through the continual pressure of particular apologetic concerns, the focus of evangelical interest keeps shifting away from the humanity of Jesus. Where does it rest instead? In a sense it moves to his divinity, though, to be more precise, it tends to focus on the supernatural elements in his divine-human person. In another sense, the failure of the humanity of Jesus to attract serious theological interest has the final result of distracting our attention from Jesus altogether–at least, from

Jesus as an historical man.

For it is *as* a man that he is presented to us in the pages of the New Testament. The tendency is to focus not on Jesus at all, as the historical New Testament figure who is so plainly–indisputably–human; but, instead, under the distorting influence of apologetics, to devise a mythical figure, whose supernatural character blots out his humanity, and who hovers between earth and heaven. In the popular imagination there can be no doubt that such an idea of Jesus is commonly held, but it is not confined to the uneducated Christian. The preacher is constantly confronted with the temptation to avert his eyes from the humanness of Christ, and to present the congregation with a Jesus whose human experience is ambivalent. As we have suggested, the focus on the death of Jesus is partly a reflection of this ambivalence, despite its (very proper) justification on other grounds. The evangelical imagination is in continual difficulty in grasping the mystery of the incarnation.

The mythical Jesus who so often and so easily surfaces is less difficult to grasp, and more congenial, since he knows less of the divine humiliation which marks the story of incarnation from beginning to end. He is the Jesus whom we cannot imagine to have been 'really' hungry, or angry, or ignorant, or in two minds, or tempted, or surprised. And that is why, despite Shedd's confident assertion, we cannot finally say that his humanity is 'undisputed'. It is true that it is undisputed in the world outside. It is equally true that it is undisputed by the liberals inside the church, for whom it is–in practice and sometimes in theory–all that there is to Jesus.

But it is only partly true of those whose understanding of Jesus seeks to be orthodox. It is their formal conviction, but it may be little more. The pressure of the apologetic agenda combines with a natural desire to resolve the complexity of the gospel portrait of Jesus into one more readily assimilable by the popular imagination. Just as the liberal tends to do this by squeezing out the supernatural, the evangelical reacts by passing over the 'natural' and emphasising what is abnormal. The supernatural model of the historical Jesus which results is an effective denial of his humanity. It is the constant tendency of orthodox Christian belief about the person of Jesus to slip into an unorthodox denial of his human nature.

What then is the effect of this neglect, and implicit denial, of the humanity of our Lord? In the chapters which follow we argue that the image which we have of Jesus Christ is crucial for the image we have of ourselves. The imitation of Christ, whether conscious or not, is part of the motivation and understanding of the Christian life. Emphasising the supernatural in Jesus has had the effect of making him superhuman, and helped an analogous process take place in our understanding of ourselves. The 'supernaturalising' of Jesus has helped lead to the supernaturalising of the Christian life. Our dissatisfaction with Jesus' humanity has led to a dissatisfaction with our own, for we have moved from a superhuman image of Jesus to a superhuman image of what is both required of the Christian and possible for him. It is only by recovering the true humanity of Jesus that we shall begin to re-discover the humanity to which we have all been called in him.

CHAPTER TWO

Was Jesus Human?

This seemingly straightforward question penetrates to the heart of the twin debates which are addressed in this book. For, with the single exception of sin, it is our humanity that Jesus has taken on himself. So it is in his sinless humanity we find the pattern for ours today. That he was indeed human is something that we take for granted. As we saw in the last chapter, it is perhaps the one doctrine which is today formally 'undisputed', both inside and outside the church. But informally, as we suggested, the matter is not so simple.

There is a deep-seated tendency to play down Jesus' humanity. It arises partly from the high place apologetics must occupy in the thinking of evangelical Christians today. Its fruit is an informal denial of the humanity of Jesus as it is portrayed in the pages of the New Testament. And it reflects the ancient formal denial which is known by the name of *docetism*. The docetic view was that Jesus only *seemed* to be human (which is what the term means), and while in an extreme form it was confined to the earliest days of the church, the docetic principle is broader. So the Dutch theologian, G.C. Berkouwer, can write that one can be a docetist and somehow 'detract from Christ's humanity' while still 'speaking of a genuine human nature'. (*The Person of Christ*, Grand Rapids, 1974, p. 198)

Conversely, merely affirming that there was an historical person called Jesus of Nazareth is not enough to resist the charge of docetism. Indeed, 'the acknowledgement of his historicity is not *half* of the Christological dogma'. This may surprise some Christians, since the general assumption behind much half-hearted and unexamined orthodoxy is just that: that the humanity of Christ implies his historicity, no less and no more. The contrast between Berkouwer and Shedd (quoted in the last chapter) is striking, for Berkouwer's chapter on the humanity of Christ is actually longer than that on his divinity. He proves to be alive to the significance of this issue, and writes that, 'despite the practically general agreement on the historicity of Jesus...the human nature of Christ remains of critical importance'.

The New Testament is emphatic in its insistence that this is so, and gives no support to the notion that humanity could ever be thought to equal mere historicity. Jesus' human nature is a positive quality which is seen as integral to the apostolic Gospel. Perhaps the most striking statement of the 'critical importance' of Jesus' humanity lies in I John, where some kind of docetic thinking is plainly in view. 'By this you know the Spirit of God', writes John. 'Every spirit which confesses that Jesus Christ has come in the flesh is of God, and every spirit which does not confess Jesus is not of God. This is the spirit of antichrist,' he goes on, 'of which you heard that it was coming, and now it is in the world already' (I John 4:2,3). Here we find an acceptance of the humanity of Jesus as the touchstone of authentic Christian testimony. By contrast, the absence of such testimony is evidence that the spirit 'is not of God'. The matter could hardly be more critical than that!

And the reason is clear: the humanity of Jesus Christ is essential to the incarnation. Anything less than a full acceptance of the one is an implicit denial of the other. The threat which docetism always poses—whether full-blown or merely implicit—is as fundamental a threat to the integrity of the Christian revelation as there could be. It is ironical that the motive of every attempt to supernaturalise Jesus Christ is so seemingly laudable: to preserve him from those who would 'naturalise' him as a mere man, and thereby deny his divine nature. This certainly makes it difficult to deal with docetism, especially in its milder forms, since it does not seem to those who believe it that it is anything other than orthodox.

Yet such an approach is deeply flawed, since it fails to accept the testimony of Scripture itself. It sets up its own criteria of what is and is not possible to God, of what is proper to him and what he can do and be. And it is finally undermined by that same New Testament evidence, since not only full-blown docetism but also the insidious, unconscious variety common among today's evangelicals is explicitly repudiated by the apostles' own witness to Jesus, the Word made flesh.

Let us look at some of this evidence, which abundantly illustrates the underlining in I John 4:2 of the fundamental conviction that Jesus Christ has come 'in the flesh'. It falls into two parts: the testimony of the gospels as to the actual human character of the life of our Lord; and the testimony of other parts of the New Testament, where, as in I John, stress is laid on that humanity and its theological significance. There can be no doubt that the temptation to move toward a docetic view of Jesus was strong, especially among those who had not known him 'in the flesh'. It was natural that they should seek to interpret the life of this man whom they believed to be the Son of God in a manner which emphasised his supernatural character. It is hardly surprising that some went beyond such an emphasis, concluding that it would have been unfitting for the Son of God to undergo the kind of human experience which a thoroughgoing humanity would imply.

But the believers of the first generation, for whom the contrast between Jesus' historical humanity and the deity which they came to predicate of him must have been greatest, were unable to eradicate their first hand knowledge of Jesus' genuine human life. In historical terms it was undoubtedly this fact of first hand apostolic testimony and authority which held the line against error. They were therefore forced to devise categories which would enable them to grasp the fact that both divine and human natures were to be found in Jesus. And though it would be several hundred years before the church could resolve its discussion of these things, it is evident that already in the New Testament documents the ground-rules for that discussion (as for every subsequent discussion) had already been laid. The testimony of the apostles, founded in their experience and reflection, has rightly been considered normative in determining the church's understanding of Jesus.

The gospels paint a telling portrait of Jesus which is remarkable for the candour with which it exposes his humanity. This judgement is underlined by two suggestive observations. The humanity of Jesus–his commonality of being and experience with us–is nowhere more evident than in the two least likely places in the gospels. The first is the Gospel of John, where there is the most explicit interest in his divine character, and yet a striking emphasis on aspects of his humanity. The second is the period recorded in all four narratives when, after the resurrection and before his ascension, we meet a Jesus who is no less human than before.

What these examples forcibly suggest is that the New Testament does not share our expectation that there will be parts of the story of Jesus that are 'more' human, and parts that are 'less'. Some of it is more supernatural in character, certainly. But the story is entirely human: and entirely divine. By seeking 'less' humanity where we expect to find 'more' divinity we reveal our failure to grasp the way the incarnation works, since at every point–in Mary's womb as much as in the temple courts, and Gethsemane, and on the cross–Jesus is divine, and human, through and through. There is no question of either the divine or the human nature somehow rivalling the other or threatening to elbow it out.

This means, of course, that there is no easy harmony of the two natures. We are grappling with a subject which is larger than our minds, and which they should not expect to be able to subdue. But it also means that we can interpret the gospel narrative freely, without constantly glancing over our shoulder to see whether what the text appears to be saying can actually be true. The gospel testimony to the human life of Jesus is meant to be just that, and was first penned and believed by those who had reached the startling conclusion that we also have reached: that this human life was the personal life of the Son of God.

A handful of examples must suffice. We can hardly paint a portrait here of the human life of Jesus, but we can indicate some of the materials from which such a picture would have to be drawn. The gospel narratives go far beyond testimony to his mere historicity, and the candour with which they do so is sometimes startling in its authenticity. We find illustrated the life of a man whose humanity, far from being invested with another quality than our own, is recognisably that of one of us. Neither his sinlessness nor his divinity has the effect–which might have been expected, and which many Christians evidently believe in the face of the evidence–of draining him of the characteristics of the humanity we know.

How do we set out to assess his humanity? It is customary to discern three areas in human consciousness: the intellectual (knowing), the emotional (feeling) and the volitional (willing). To these we may add a fourth: the bodily form in which this consciousness is to be found. No doubt other ways could be found of setting out the constituent parts of human nature, but for our present purposes this is as good as any. The experience, capacities and characteristics of *Homo sapiens* fall into these four basic categories. What they do not include is any recognition of man's spiritual nature, but for reasons which will be further considered later in our discussion we leave that question aside. That is not because it can be neglected, but rather out of respect for its fundamental character. Man's spirituality is not simply another aspect of his humanity, to be set alongside these four. It is another dimension, which pervades the whole and which cannot be set over against or distinguished from the bodily, intellectual, emotional and volitional character of man.

The bodily character of Jesus is hardly in doubt, and only in ancient full-blown docetism was it actually denied. Our difficulty is that it is common to see Jesus' corporeality as the sum and substance of the incarnation, as if only in actually possessing a body was Jesus like us. The stress in the gospels on the corporeal character of Jesus' life is sometimes taken to suggest this mistakenly limited view of incarnation. Yet stress there certainly is. Not only is the fundamental statement of the incarnation couched in the terms that 'the Word became flesh', but the particulars of family tree, conception and delivery are spelled out so as to underline the natural human origins and therefore human nature of this human child–notwithstanding the miraculous elements in the process by which incarnation takes place. The account of the twelve-year old Jesus in the temple, though scant material for the biographer, is a vital link in the human story of his growth in wisdom and stature, welding the accounts of birth and manhood with its cameo of the adolescent Jesus with a distinctive and growing religious consciousness.

The ministry of Jesus, which forms so large a portion of the gospels, is presented to us as the ministry of a man who gets hungry and thirsty, and eats and drinks; who tires, and rests and sleeps; who seeks time alone and for prayer, away from the crowds and away also from his friends. And though the death of Jesus is so much more, it is nothing less than the death of a man. Jesus is born, and Jesus dies. The gospel tells the lifestory of a man, and even after he is raised–as we have pointed out–the bodily elements are almost embarrassingly present: 'Put your finger here, and see my hands; and put out your hand, and place it in my side' (John 20:27).

The question of the intellectual life of our Lord is one that is shrouded in mystery, since here more than anywhere else we see the divine and the human in union. But there are nevertheless elements to which our attention is drawn by the gospels. We note the enormous intellectual power of Jesus, in his uniquely creative use of parable and in his strikingly effective public debates with his religious opponents. Though it is not common for us to consider Jesus' human mind, it is plain that he had massive intellectual gifts. His qualities as a teacher are more commonly discussed, but it is important to recognise that he was no mere educator in other men's ideas.

We should also note the vital role which his knowledge of the Old Testament evidently played in the development of his religious self-consciousness and the fundamental theological convictions which run throughout his teaching. It is clear that a creative synthesis of his own profound study of Scripture was, in human terms, the source of his distinctive teaching. The fact that his human knowledge was gained by natural means is illustrated by the occasions on which he asks questions, expresses surprise and disappointment, and by the famous occasion on which he expresses ignorance of the time of the Second Coming.

This last suggests, among other things, that his religious knowledge was also generally gained by natural means; at least (and this may be an important distinction) by the means whereby other men gain their own religious knowledge. Where it concerns existential questions rather than simply matters of information it is unlikely that we can describe these means as simply 'natural', save in the sense that they are natural to the religious man and elements in his normal human experience.

How we properly account for and describe that experience is a complex question. It is hard to see how it can be explained simply in terms of a naturalistic nexus of cause and effect. The 'natural' religious life of the Christian is constantly also 'supernatural', in that normal religious activities such as prayer and worship bring him directly into contact with the personal God. In that sense, Jesus' religious life, as presented in the gospels, appears intriguingly to have taken a course which was fundamentally analogous with that of other men. As a boy, he asked questions; as a man, he prayed, he wrestled repeatedly with temptation, his human spirit shrank from the darkness which awaited him.

The question of Jesus' will is complex, but it is hard to avoid the conclusion that he did not find it any easier to make right choices than did any other man. The twin facts of his sinlessness and his temptation tend to suggest that he faced a struggle in the taking of right decisions which eclipses the moral struggles of mere sinners. The wilderness temptation narrative leaves us in no doubt that the agony of resisting evil and choosing good was a true part of his human experience.

It is sometimes suggested that because his nature was such that he could not concede, the experience of temptation would be a matter of indifference; yet, on the contrary–and as the narrative itself indicates–since every time he had to secure a victory, and could not take refuge in defeat, his was the greatest struggle engaged by man with the forces of darkness. For each of us, there are temptations which have little power, and may be simply resisted; and there are others which catch us where we are most vulnerable. If our character is such that to submit to them would deny all we know ourselves to be, the struggle can be sore, however inevitable the outcome might seem after the event. We return to this question in the final chapter.

Alongside the narrative of the wilderness temptations there is one other which speaks to us specially of the will of Jesus, and that is the harrowing tale of Gethsemane. It is plain from this account that Jesus faces the prospect of the cross with almost unbelievable anguish. Despite the events in the Upper Room, he appears unprepared and unwilling to face what he knows lies ahead. It is striking how he actually prays that, if possible, the cup might pass from him.

This is a very remarkable statement, for its candour and its humility; and its open access into the totally human character of Jesus. It is, perhaps, the most deadly blow to be struck by the New Testament itself against every kind of docetism. For it reveals Jesus' commitment, his entire existential engagement in his mission, the wholly realistic character of his human experience. There is no *seeming* here; there is rather the raw, exposed integrity of human being.

And there is emotion! The emotional life of Jesus throbs with such moments of self-disclosure in the vortex of human pain. 'Jesus wept', we read, at the tomb of Lazarus his friend. He sighs, he is distressed, he has pity and compassion, he weeps over Jerusalem. Moreover, he shows anger (sometimes fiercely) and indignation; and love, and joy.

In a famous essay on this theme, the great American theologian Benjamin B. Warfield writes of the profound character of these emotional experiences recorded in the gospels. Jesus knew 'not mere joy but exultation, not mere irritated annoyance but raging indignation, not mere passing pity but the deepest movements of compassion and love, not mere surface distress but an exceeding sorrow even unto death', yet all without their mastering him, all without sin. And Warfield goes on to quote Calvin: 'the Son of God having clothed himself with our flesh, of his own accord also clothed himself with human feelings, so that he did not differ at all from his brethren, sin only excepted.' ('The Emotional Life of our Lord', *Person and Work of Christ*, Philadelphia, 1950, pp. 142f)

From this brief survey of the evidence of the gospels we turn to a further example of the New Testament's reflection upon the human life of Jesus. Perhaps most striking of all is the discussion of his priestly role in the letter to the Hebrews, the more telling in its emphasis upon his humanity since the context of this discussion is that of the conscious elevation of Christ above every creature: 'When he had made purification for sins, he sat down at the right hand of the Majesty on high, having become as much superior to angels as the name he has obtained is more excellent than theirs' (Hebrews 1:3,4).

The letter to the Hebrews stresses not simply the fact, but the necessity, of our Lord's experience of the human condition. 'Since...the children share in flesh and blood, he himself likewise partook of the same nature, that through death he might destroy him who has the power of death' (2:14). 'Therefore he had to be made like his brethren in every respect, so that he might become a merciful and faithful high priest' (2:17). Again, Jesus' sympathy with our weaknesses derives from his being 'one who in every respect has been tempted as we are, yet without sin' (4:15). This in turn is the ground on which we may approach him, 'that we may receive mercy and find grace to help in time of need' (4:16). The human experience of Jesus is then graphically summarised: 'In the days of his flesh, Jesus offered up prayers and supplications, with loud cries and tears, to him who was able to save him from death, and he was heard for his godly fear' (5:7).

So we find, set unashamedly alongside each other, the high dignity of the Son of God and the actual, historical experience of Jesus of Nazareth. Both alike are set in their theological perspective. The writer feels no need to comment on the sharpness of these contrasts, since he does not see himself working under any constraint to harmonise them. His purpose is to speak of the humanity of Jesus and its context in his ascended glory and the glorious purposes for which it was ordained.

Here more than anywhere else in the New Testament, we find blunt acknowledgement of the raw material provided by the gospel narratives, and a picture of Jesus in his humiliation as a man partaking 'of flesh and blood', 'made like his brethren in every respect' apart from sin. It is a defiantly human picture of Jesus.

And there is no other picture. The Biblical witness is clear. It cuts through our continued attempts to dull the sharpness of its language and muzzle its message, and affirms repeatedly the oneness of Jesus and his brothers, alike partakers in flesh and blood.

What underlies this is the conviction that Jesus was not *incidentally* human, but deliberately, necessarily, thoroughly. And by taking our nature to himself he has set a divine seal upon human life. If we seek to understand our humanity we must do so henceforward with one eye upon his. He it is who had led the normative human life, the single life that has resisted sin; and offered to God the perfect sacrifice–which we never can–of a life obedient to the Father at every point. Not only so. By taking human life into the very godhead, he has hallowed human existence and asserted afresh and forever the worth and the dignity of bearing the image of God.

Not that this dignity stems from the incarnation. It is right at the beginning that 'God created man in his own image, in the image of God he created him; male and female he created them' (Genesis 1:27). The very possibility of the incarnation of the Son of God itself rests on our possession of the image. It is because man fundamentally reflects the personal character of God that God himself can take on flesh and blood. We can make sense of incarnation only in the light of what we know already about the constitution of man as the highest of all the creatures of God, whom God has made for fellowship with himself. The high dignity which this confers upon human existence is radically underscored by the union of divine and human natures in Jesus Christ. God commits himself to us forever by clothing his own Son with human nature.

It is clear, therefore, how deeply we err if we seek to minimise the significance or, as it were, the extent of the incarnation. The picture of a Jesus who cannot be imagined as undergoing authentic human experience is a myth of our own devising, the product of a supernaturalising of the story and its interpretation. Not only is it unfaithful to the New Testament record itself (both in the gospels and elsewhere), but it reveals itself as basically out of sympathy with the divine intention to take flesh and blood. God's purpose in incarnation is precisely to take upon himself the gamut of human experience, sin alone apart. His identification with our human condition is total.

One of our difficulties is that this may puzzle us, since our minds are unable to grasp the manner in which it could come about. At the same time, it should fill us with awe, that God should so dignify human nature as to make it his own. But it is not improper, it is no matter of shame. For though in our sin we are rebels deserving only the censure and judgement of God, in our human state apart from sin–that human experience into which Jesus entered–we are the glory of the entire creation. We are made like him, as like him as any creature could be made; and we are made for him, for fellowship with him to all eternity. The real marvel of incarnation is not that God should become man, but that he should do so *for us men and for our salvation*. At the end of the day, it is not chiefly a marvel of the mind, but a marvel of the heart.

The question with which we began was *Was Jesus Human?* Perhaps it could have been better put, since it implies that he *is* human no longer–that his humanity was confined to his years in Palestine, and laid aside when the period of his humiliation came to an end in ascension and exaltation.

But this is not so. Neglected even more than the historic humanity of Jesus in Palestine is his present and continuing humanity in glory. The ascended and glorified Saviour retains his human nature even in his exalted state. If it were possible, this still further stresses the high dignity of those who bear the image of God. And the entire identity, human and divine, of Jesus of Nazareth and the exalted Saviour sheds new light on the sympathy and compassion of 'our great high priest, who has passed through the heavens' (Hebrews 4:14). This extraordinary and widely disregarded implication of the doctrine of the incarnation is actually central to our understanding of God.

Charles Hodge, perhaps the greatest evangelical theologian of the nineteenth century, expressed this fact memorably in his massive *Systematic Theology*. 'We have all the advantage of his human sympathy and affection,' Hodge writes, 'and the form of divine life which we derive from Him comes from Him as God still clothed in our nature' (vol. 2, p. 634). For 'this supreme ruler of the universe is a perfect man as well as a perfect God'. So 'it is, therefore, at the feet of a man in whom dwells the fulness of the Godhead, that all principalities and powers bow themselves in willing subjection and adoring love' (p. 637). And the hymn-writers have also expressed it well. In 'Crown him with many crowns', we sing of:

> *Rich wounds yet visible above,*
> *In beauty glorified.*

Perhaps most strikingly of all, Charles Wesley, whose hymns speak so powerfully of the human nature of the Christian, closes his Christmas hymn 'Glory be to God on high' with the following stanza:

> *We, the sons of men, rejoice,*
> *The Prince of Peace proclaim;*
> *With Heaven's host lift up our voice,*
> *And shout Immanuel's name:*
> *Knees and hearts to Him we bow,*
> *Of our flesh and of our bone,*
> *Jesus is our brother now,*
> *And God is all our own.*

The dignity of human nature, fashioned in the divine image, is such that God can take it for himself—and keep it. The 'supreme ruler of the universe is a perfect man as well as a perfect God': Jesus is our brother now.

CHAPTER THREE

Faith and the Mind

We suggested in the last chapter that a convenient way of assessing human nature was to conceive it under four categories. Man has a mind: he thinks, there is an intellectual aspect that is fundamental to his human being. Secondly, the volitional: he has a will, he makes decisions. Thirdly, man is an emotional creature: he has feelings. Fourthly, and most basically, he is a physical being: he has a body. We briefly examined the humanity of Jesus under each of these headings. And we suggested that, in his case as in ours, it would be misleading to see the spiritual character of human existence as simply a further aspect in this list. Rather, it should be considered another dimension of human nature, underlying all of these and relating to them in their constitution of man, the bearer of the image of God.

In this and the three following chapters we turn our attention to the way in which evangelicals understand the Christian life. The argument is as follows. Our lack of interest in the humanity of Jesus, partly explained by the influence of apologetics on our understanding of the Christian faith, has encouraged a situation in which many Christians find being human to be a growing embarrassment. In one way or another they feel they must somehow rise above it.

As a result, we face subtle and pernicious influences that seek to undermine our confidence in every area of human experience. There is nothing which is left untouched. Our thinking, our willing, our feeling and our very physical constitution are all questioned. And though these influences are of different kinds, they hold in common an implicit dissatisfaction with our calling to be *men and women* in Christ, and a desire to be something more than human. There could be no better antidote than a recovery of the neglected but glorious doctrine of the unashamed humanity of Jesus Christ, who though he was divine took to himself a perfect but unadorned human nature, and who wears it still.

For all their differences, a pattern emerges in each of the following cases. There is a distortion, an imbalance which, while claiming to stress what is good, results in a fatal disturbance of the truth. Something is emphasised in such a way as to deny other things that are true. In the process, it ceases to be true. For when truth is exaggerated it does not become some kind of super-truth. So much evangelical thinking is seriously flawed by its insistence on this principle. What happens is that exaggerated truth becomes sub-truth, and sub-truth is falsehood.

So a distorted, exaggerated notion of faith leads to the denial of reason. An exaggerated idea of divine guidance distorts our understanding of Christian responsibility. An over-emphasis on self-control and *sangfroid* effectively denies that man is an emotional creature. A naïve concept of providence can so stress God's care for the Christian as to lead him to expect to be lifted right out of the real world.

Now, as has been said, these are all matters of emphasis, and they lie in areas in which dividing lines are difficult to draw. Some of these distortions are more evident than others in particular strands of the evangelical tradition. Setting the four of them together sheds new light on the significance of each one, and it is sobering to realise that, taken together, they constitute a wholesale denial of human nature as constituted by God. That is to say, in these distortions of spiritual and theological truth, there lie the seeds of the denial of all that is true about man— save for his spiritual character, in whose name these seeds of denial are sown. So in this chapter, and the three which follow, we go in search of a balanced view of the truth of Christian living.

For balance is all-important. These distortions to which we have drawn attention, like the related distortions in our picture of Jesus, find their appeal in reaction against falsehood of another kind. We react against the idea that Jesus is merely a man, but unless we are careful we do so by, as we have said, 'supernaturalising' him and undermining the integrity of his humanity. By the same token, in reacting against the humanist who is lax about sin and uninterested in God, and unless we are careful, we do the same thing to our view of the Christian life: we seek to rise above our humanity, we create expectations and lay burdens which are undeserved, and we develop a mythical idea of Christian living in place of one that is authentic. We must not be content with such distortions of the truth. The balance must be redressed.

In this chapter we raise a number of questions. They have in common the character of man as a creature with a mind.

The Mind and Reason

There is no charge more commonly levelled against evangelical Christians than that of anti-intellectualism, and there can be little doubt that it is often justified. The error of those who bring it lies in supposing that such an attitude rightly reflects the character of evangelical religion. They suppose that a repudiation of the intellect is required, since otherwise the religion will be incredible. Needless to say, this supposition has proved convenient, since it carries the implication that the claims of evangelical religion are not worthy of serious intellectual consideration. No doubt that explains why some people are so ready to bring this charge, and accuse evangelicals of requiring a 'sacrifice of the intellect' before an intelligent person could be expected to swallow what they believe.

Yet there is much in evangelical attitudes to the use of the mind which justifies such a view. It is all too common to hear 'faith' set over against the mind, the intellect, the reason, as if it were an independent and alternative entity in the make-up of the Christian. One reason for this–which causes confusion both on the part of Christians and of their critics–is the consequence of different uses of the idea of 'reason'.

The human reason is a tool for sorting out our perception of reality, and as such plays a humble but essential role in the lives of us all. This is so not merely for those of us who realise what is going on: it is impossible to function as a human being without using your faculty to reason. Problems arise when the status of the reason is raised, and we move from the idea of rational*ity* (*i.e.*, reasonableness) to that of rational*ism*. This is really nothing to do with the human mind itself, but is rather a theory about the human mind which declares that there is nothing beyond it. It is an anti-religious supposition.

Being 'reasonable' or 'rational' is therefore entirely different from being 'rationalistic'. Rationalism is in fact itself unreasonable, since it arbitrarily closes off any notion that there might be a God. It is also, therefore, itself a form of anti-intellectualism. We make a big mistake if, in reacting against it, we declare ourselves to be against human reason.

So the confusion of reason and rationalism is one factor which has led many Christians to downgrade the importance of their minds. Another is the defensiveness which, as we noted in Chapter 1, has been characteristic of conservative Christians during the last century. They have found that their convictions are those of only a minority within the churches. Confronted with the confident claim that 'what you believe about this, or that, is unreasonable', there are many who have responded with the simple retort, 'who cares about reason, I believe this by faith!'.

At a time when historic Christian conviction has been under growing intellectual pressure, it is perhaps inevitable that people should resort to such a defence of their beliefs. It takes both information and intellectual equipment to answer such charges. But that does not mean there are no reasonable answers, least of all that the faith-versus-reason dichotomy is necessary to evangelical belief.

As it happens, the retreat from reason in the evangelical church is more deep-seated than may appear from this example, since it is not simply in particular instances that individuals have offered this kind of response. It could be argued that a distrust of reasoning lies behind much of the weakness of evangelical thinking today, both about God and also about the world. We return to these questions later.

The crucial fact is that the human reason is inescapable, and will either be used or abused. If we think, we reason. There is no alternative route to knowledge, whether of God or his creation, and we simply deceive ourselves if we consider reasonableness to be lacking in spiritual faithfulness. God's revelation is made to, and must be apprehended by, our reasoning faculty: it is itself not least in the panoply of human gifts which mirror God himself.

The Mind and Theology

It is a striking feature of much of contemporary evangelicalism that it is little concerned with theology–in the sense of serious study, to the highest level of our ability, of God and his revelation. Of course, theology as an academic discipline has got itself a bad name. The theologians who find their way into the public gaze often do so thanks to their notoriety as heretics. The theological studies courses of our universities are often in the hands of men and women with little evangelical sympathy.

But the fact that there is much bad theology is no argument at all against evangelical engagement in theology that is good. On the contrary, it should serve as a spur to theological activity within the evangelical community. Unbiblical and unorthodox thinking about God needs to be exposed, and we must have the confidence to believe that, since historic Christianity is in fact true, we can embark on a discussion of any aspect of the faith, at any level of enquiry, believing that God will honour our work.

Of course, this does not mean that 'academic' theology is for everyone, though the principle is important that each Christian man or woman should seek to understand the faith to as great a depth as he or she is able. If we are old enough to swim, we must not be content to stay in the shallows. We must let our minds be stretched by the revelation of God, always resisting the temptation to be content when there is more we can learn. And this will involve, as well as personal openness to read and to be taught, an awareness in the wider evangelical community of the special task to which those who can engage in theological work at the highest level are called. We must ensure that there are those set aside within the evangelical community to devote time and energy to the study of the faith.

The Mind and Evangelism

What is the relation of the Christian reason and the evangelistic task of the church? Here more than anywhere else the 'faith versus reason' question is raised. As it happens, the biblical examples of evangelistic speech are striking in their rational character. An examination of Jesus' own public discourses and his handling of questions, and the addresses of Paul and Peter in the Acts of the Apostles, bears testimony to the essentially *reasonable* character of the Bible's own proclamation of the Gospel.

Of special interest is the way in which Paul addresses the Athenian philosophers on Mars Hill (in Acts 17). It is plain that the chief aim in his address to these pagans is to construct the argument which is best able to lead their minds from their present convictions to faith in Christ. So he quotes their poetry, he adverts to their unknown God, and it is from this introduction that he moves on to the resurrection and the Gospel. Paul sets out to use his mind to convince the Athenians, through their minds, of the truth of his message about God. Is there not an example there for us?

Of course, part of the lesson of the Acts is that in different places–Jerusalem and Athens, for example–evangelism will take different forms. It will be tailored to its audience. Not that the Gospel will change, but there are a thousand ways in which it can be introduced and commended to those who do not believe; and if it is to be intelligently and responsibly proclaimed, and received, they will be used.

In fact the best-argued case can prove unsuccessful, and the worst or most inappropriately presented reap rich response. There is no doubt in the New Testament that it is God who, by his Holy Spirit, provokes response to the Gospel: it is not the excellence, or otherwise, of human argument. But neither is there any doubt that, if we would pattern ourselves upon the apostles and their co-workers, we must employ all the resources of our human reason to commend the Gospel of God. Since God has made us reasonable creatures, we can do no less.

We have already noted that, albeit imperfectly and on a human scale, the human reason reflects the reason of God. It is God himself who has made us rational beings, and while we are much more than *merely* rational, we are never anything less. If we treat ourselves, or each other, as irrational, unreasoning creatures, we despise what God had given–and what, in its broken fashion, reflects his own mind.

So it is that, in the normal operation of his Spirit, he deigns to approach us through our minds. The Gospel is set out in Holy Scripture and preached to us as it was to its first hearers as a reasonable message. If we believe–as some of them believed–because the arguments are convincing, we will never be able to stop simply with a belief in the conclusions of convincing arguments. That is because their logic is self-involving:

if we believe the Gospel, we have no option but to believe 'I am a sinner, I must repent, I must seek forgiveness', for that is the message it unmistakably bears.

But it is logic nonetheless. There is no other way to read the New Testament than as a reasoned setting forth of the Gospel, tailored carefully to the needs and backgrounds of communities all across the ancient world in which it was received. We owe it to our fellow men and women, when we bring them the Gospel, to show them the human respect which Peter and Paul showed to its first hearers, and which God himself has shown to us; to present them with the best and most appropriate case for the Gospel and their belief in it.

We must approach them first of all *through their minds*. While our presentation will not be abstract but personal, as befits the character of the message, it will also deliberately seek entry to the mind by virtue of its reasonable appeal. Any other presentation will dishonour both itself and its hearers.

The Mind, Culture and Calling

The intellectual faculty of man is not limited to his powers of reasoning. Indeed, one of the curiosities of the evangelical movement is that it is sometimes accused at one and the same time of being both 'anti-intellectual' and 'rationalistic'. This stems partly from the perception that, when evangelicals do use their minds, their real interest–like that of anyone who is seeking to win converts to his way of thinking–is in particular lines of argument which arrive at predictable conclusions. Their interest in the human reason is as a means to certain religious ends. They are less likely to be interested in other uses of the mind, and there are large areas of evangelicalism in which scholarly, cultural and aesthetic endeavour is regarded, sometimes overtly, as improper.

In thus sealing off large tracts of human experience from Christian participation, it is the Christian's 'priorities' to which appeal is chiefly made, though it is sometimes suggested that there is something inherently wrong with, for example, the reading of fiction as a Christian pastime, or the writing of fiction as a Christian vocation. Though Christians have their own priorities, arguments couched in this form are usually dangerous. They can hide other kinds of (often subjective) reasoning. They tend also to prove more than they intend, if their logic is followed through. If reading fiction is a waste of time which could be better spent, what about listening to music, or reading biographies? If writing fiction is not a respectable Christian calling, what about writing music, or biography, or running a fish and chip shop?

Evangelical Christians tend to be too ready to prescribe how others ought to behave, and to judge them when they fail to conform. The moral questions on which the Bible offers its own guidance are far removed from many of the practical issues which we face. Particular cultural norms and taboos are readily–and often uncritically–established or, perhaps, assimilated in the evangelical tradition. One has only to mention such examples as going to the cinema and wearing make-up to show the disproportionate relation that can develop between the firmness with which opinions are held and their (lack of) biblical justification. And, of course, they can change with an embarrassing rapidity.

In fact, the argument about culture and priorities raises a fundamental issue that is only partly relevant to the subject of this chapter. We understand 'culture' here in a broad sense, not simply as a term for the arts but to cover the whole range of essentially human activities–work, leisure, friendship, family life, government. They are all activities of the 'mind' of man, though in its role as the guide of his whole self.

Christians take many different approaches to these questions, but there are two basic types to one or other of which they all tend to conform. According to one, the religious work of the church must take priority over everything else. 'Priority' in this case has the effect of excluding all other claims on the time and energy and money of the Christian–all claims, that is, which cannot be shown to play some part in the furthering of these religious purposes. According to the other, Christian men and women are in principle able–indeed, are called–to engage in legitimate cultural activity of one kind and another, including that which *cannot* be shown to have any direct connection with the religious purposes of the church.

Now, this description of these basic cultural types can no doubt be faulted, but they do present two fundamentally different approaches to the question of the Christian life. That does not mean that we should always expect an evident difference in lifestyle between adherents of the first and second groups. It is a matter of motive, and how people seek to understand–and justify–their behaviour. There are also norms and conventions which have been established within particular communities. And, of course, there are the large inconsistencies of which people can so easily be guilty. Yet, when these factors are recognised, the broad outlines of these two views are seen to be distinct.

It could be argued that going to the opera is a way of meeting people who can then be evangelised; or that being well-read is a necessary pre-requisite to getting to know such people before the Gospel can be offered them. So people from both groups are found doing the same things, even though there are many things which those in the first group will be much less likely to be found doing; partly because they may be inclined to suspect sophistry in an argument like that. But there are meeting-points at which both these principles could be genuinely brought together.

So it might be argued that being *disinterestedly* engaged in cultural activity better enables one to engage in evangelism and other religious activities. Or, perhaps most important of all, that instead of seeking 'religious' advantages to be had from engaging in what we are broadly calling 'cultural' activities, we ought properly to extend the scope of the 'religious' category so as to include rather more of human experience than, say, worship and evangelism. To take this further: we might suggest that there is something improper about the division of human activity into 'religious' and 'other' which is presupposed by our analysis–and, in particular, by those who fall into our first category.

For the question is, what does the Lord our God require of us? It could hardly be more fundamental. What has he set us here to do and to be? In line with some of the facetious questions we have already used to take us into this discussion, we might ask, *What are Christians for?* The answers are basically two in number, in line with the division we have already noted. There are those who consider that Christians are called to engage exclusively in religious activity: the preaching of the Gospel, the building up of the church, and similar matters. Everything else that they do must be justified on the grounds of the contribution it makes to this task: family, job, use of spare time, money, and so on.

And there are those who take another perspective altogether. They find their starting-point in our calling as Christians who have been made in the image of God. Redemption is not the whole of the story. We begin where the Bible begins, with the creation of man and with God's first declaration of his purposes to men and women in the beginning, 'let them have dominion' (Genesis 1:26).

This charter for the human race commands man to *be* man, the prince of God's world, his steward over the immense resources at the disposal of the human race. The consequence of man's disobedience and fall has been grave, but, just as it has not erased the image of God which he bears, so the mandate of God's purposes remains. The long story of redemption, with its glorious climax in his taking human flesh to himself and finally dying in the place of his rebellious creature–that story does not supplant the original purposes of God. Rather, it enables them to be fulfilled, in a manner more splendid than could at first have been imagined.

Never is there any retraction of God's fundamental purpose for man: dominion of the earth for God. Never is it suggested that, henceforth, he is to be a merely, narrowly, religious creature. The move from the vision and purpose of Genesis 1 to the first principle set out in our discussion above could hardly be greater. The redemptive, 'religious' calling of the Christian is to be set within the broader context of creation. To put it better, there is no final conflict between the 'religious' goals of the first principle and the broader concerns enshrined in the second principle, since true religion, the religion of the Bible, embraces them both.

What are Christians for? We are to be religious, in the specific sense of serving God in the church and witnessing to him in the world; but we are also to be human, living redeemed lives in God's world and fulfilling his first purposes for creation. So whether we are clergy or golf caddies, whether we relax by reading (or earn our living by writing) missionary biographies or detective stories, whether we seek out our neighbours so as to bring them to church or simply with disinterested friend-ship and joy in their company—we do it for God and as stewards of his world.

By contrast, those who seek to narrow their obligations and the purposes of God to 'religious' activity confine the sphere of his concerns to the church alone. By locking him into the church, they lock him out of his world; and they relegate that world—the natural order as well as the world of men—to a lowly place. It is as if they seek to deny that the Christian is 'in the world' at all.

There are several points at which these rival views of the Christian life come to a focus. One is in the family, and the priority which Christians will be prepared to give to family responsibilities as over against those of the church and other religious involvements. There are Christians who shamefully neglect their families in the supposed interest of the work of God. This is a broader question than can be given an adequate discussion here, but we should note that in our family commitments we have responsibilities which are not directly linked to the 'religious' concerns of evangelism and worship, and yet which are generally agreed to *be* responsibilities.

That is to say, marriage vows and parental obligations are not to be seen as subservient to church commitments. They stand in their own right. We can face difficult decisions in the conflicting demands which religious and family obligations can make. Yet the argument that family must 'come second' to church commitments is a naïve alternative to the careful balancing of time and resources which is our Christian duty.

The tension becomes clearer in the related area of vocation. For there is a deep-seated ambivalence in many evangelical circles about 'secular' work. It is sometimes viewed as just a way of earning a living and enabling someone to give support to the work of the church, in time and giving. There are half-way house occupations, such that in the case of doctors, nurses, teachers and some others, a 'vocational' element is more obvious. But even these are firmly divided from the distinctively 'religious' calling of ministers and missionaries. We need to recover a sense of the secular world as a place which is fit for Christian vocation, whether that of the doctor or of the novelist, the politician, the manual labourer or the housewife. These are all alike honourable callings for the Christian. They require no special justification.

In a typical evangelical congregation, there will be a strong tendency to focus interest and prayer quite disproportionately on those who are engaged in overtly religious activity. Those engaged in other kinds of work will tend to attract interest chiefly in 'religious' areas: teachers if they teach RE, office workers in their Christian fellowship meetings, as if God's interest in his world was suddenly confined to religious activity.

Yet the secretary is called by God to be just that, and to serve him in the service of his or her employer; and so for the road-mender, and the signalman, and the member of the Cabinet. They are not performing these vital functions merely *incidentally*, in order–for example–that they might invite their colleagues to church. Their prime responsibility to God is for the manner in which they conduct their vocation. Adam's calling was as a gardener. And Jesus', for the greater part of his life, as a carpenter. These secular vocations were their principal spheres of service.

We might be happier in denying that there *are* 'secular' vocations, and–as we have already suggested–extending our notion of what is 'religious' to encompass everything that man is called to be and to do. We would then have a concept of proper, religious vocation ('religious' in the more specific sense as well as secular) and improper, irreligious, distinctly sinful activity. There is employment which must surely fall in such a category, though we need to draw our conclusions here with unusual case. No doubt some Christians would regard the management of a cinema or theatre as self-evidently falling into such a category, or employment in a restaurant or supermarket which sold alcohol. Yet we are called to be 'in the world', and not simply 'in the church'. We cannot escape from the fallen structures which now make up God's world. The option of withdrawal is not an option, and those who have sought to take it have only deceived themselves.

God did not boycott his fallen world, and nor must we. There is neither religious nor secular to God, but one world over which we have been called to have dominion.

George Herbert's poem so beautifully expresses the lordship of God in the common and the secular as in the holy:

Teach me, my God and King,
In all things thee to see,
And what I do in anything,
To do it as for thee!...

All may of thee partake;
Nothing could be so mean,
Which with this tincture, 'for thy sake',
Will not grow bright and clean.

A servant with this clause
Makes drudgery divine:
Who sweeps a room, as for thy laws,
Makes that and th'action fine.

This is the famous stone,
That turneth all to gold;
For that which God doth touch and own
Cannot for less be told.

Herbert calls this poem 'The Elixir': the secret potion of the alchemists which they supposed would turn all to gold. The elixir of the common life of humankind is 'for thy sake', and with it on our lips and in our hearts God sends us out into his world to live for him.

CHAPTER FOUR

Guidance and the Will

Some of the most difficult theological and spiritual problems faced by Christians focus on the question of 'guidance'–how we know what God wants us to do. This is no wonder. In our individual spiritual experience, the same question keeps recurring. What should I be doing? What do I do next? Is this course of action right? From the perspective of theology it is equally central, since the goal of the Christian life is to do the will of God. Adam fell when he decided to disobey God. Jesus came to bring the remedy of forgiveness and, with the empowering of the Holy Spirit, a new ability to obey. So there can be no more pressing question than the discovery of what the divine will is for us, and how we may discern it.

So it is no surprise that ideas of guidance lie at the heart of evangelical life and experience. What is perhaps surprising is that they are so little discussed. They are communicated through the sharing of experiences, and the deductions we draw from them; or, perhaps, the assumptions on which we have acted and which we have found to work. Evangelical theology, partly as a result of its preoccupation with apologetics, has spent little time in systematic reflection on the Christian life. That is no doubt one reason why a kind of orthodoxy has been able to develop in some circles, largely unchallenged, which raises serious questions.

There is another reason, and this doubtless helps account for the lack of formal discussion. The subject of divine guidance is one that cuts to the heart of our personal experience of God, and the way in which we interpret that experience. It is therefore one of the most delicate and potentially embarrassing of all subjects. Each of us has much invested in the outcome. For we all have our own ideas about guidance: we have all sought it, found it, followed it, and based much upon our confidence that we have been right–not just in the decisions we have made, but in the way in which we have made them.

So this chapter deals with potentially fragile material, and we must point out that it is not our intention to call in question individual experiences of the guiding hand of God. There are exceptions, there are special cases, where–in the narratives recorded in Holy Scripture as in the stories of our own lives–God is pleased to act in a distinctive and extraordinary fashion. That we cannot doubt. The question we ask is of a different kind. How may we normally *expect* him to act? To put it another way, and to return to the issue with which we began, how do we decide what we should do next?

Of course, there are different kinds of decision, and some are resolved simply. There are basic ethical issues on which the the Bible gives its own guidance: adultery, theft and murder are wrong, and helping someone in difficulty is an obligation. And there are decisions which (from a religious or ethical perspective) are generally agreed to be trivial, and on which no kind of divine instruction would be expected to be sought: what colour of wallpaper do we choose for the living room? Shall we go to the park or the museum today?

Seemingly trivial questions may themselves reflect broader decisions about lifestyle which are definitely ethical ones. Should I make a point of spending one day a week with the children going somewhere like the park or the museum? Ought we to re-decorate the house so often, even though we can afford to? But the point is this: there are two basic kinds of decision-making on which we are all agreed. There are fundamental ethical norms which settle fundamental ethical questions. And there are (ethically) trivial questions on which we simply have to make up our own minds.

Problems begin to arise when we consider decisions which lie between these two, and the area between them is a large one. It includes basic lifetime choices about marriage (both whether and who), vocation, church membership and so forth. And it includes less significant matters–everything else, indeed, that is not (like the wallpaper and the park) plainly trivial and of no particular ethical or religious consequence.

We cannot hope in this chapter to suggest a comprehensive understanding of this subject, and we may raise more questions than we can answer. What we intend to do is to discuss some aspects of the question in the light of the humanity of the Christian. In a nutshell, our argument is that many evangelicals have come to assume a perspective on Christian decision-making which effectively denies that Christians are called upon to make decisions at all. It fails adequately to recognise their integrity and responsibility.

It is not difficult to characterise the most extreme pattern of 'guidance' thinking, though some will think this to be caricature. Probably more widespread than we might imagine, in the secret and often only half-formed understanding of many Christians, this idea of guidance exercises a powerful pull on others, since it seems to offer a coherent concept of how to discern the mind of God for our own, particular circumstances.

Of course, there is much in this pattern which is by no means to be despised. It consists of good elements and bad, a curate's egg of popular theology; and those who believe it–to whatever degree–do so with conscientious piety, which we gladly respect. But sincerity and piety do not of themselves guarantee truth; while a mistaken approach, here as in the case of evangelism (which we discussed in the last chapter), does not guarantee error. If we honestly seek to determine the will of God for our own circumstances by the throwing of dice, we may be foolish, we may even be doing something positively evil, but it is always possible that in his grace and goodness God will use this curious method to show us what to do.

The same may be said, the more so, for the more common idea we are discussing. The crucial point is this: as in the throwing of dice, God *may* choose to concur in our scheme. He *may* choose to unravel his will through these means, though we have no reason to believe that he should. He may well not. So our method is flawed: it may, and it may not, lead us to an understanding of the will of God. Conscience and piety notwithstanding, it might equally lead us in the opposite direction.

The common idea of guidance which we have called 'extreme'–or Guidance, with a capital G–runs something like this. If we seek to know what to do, if a decision is required of us, we come to God in prayer, we clear our minds, and we listen for his voice. This theory is often combined with others: being on the look-out for coincidences (we hear three times in quick succession about a town in Africa: are we being called to go there?); sticking pins in texts or taking promises out of boxes. We could add other common ideas, and we are not suggesting that they are all to be rejected. Some may have a real role to play in our making of Christian decisions.

The point is this: they do not provide us with a foolproof formula by which we can determine the will of God. Whatever role they have, it cannot be that one. And the first idea we mentioned–the emptying of the mind in prayer–is profoundly suspect. Not that illumination is forbidden to us in the course of prayer, or that God may not sometimes speak to us with great directness; but this is not a formula, and we shall come unstuck if we try to use it as if it were.

By focussing on the extreme view, which would use some combination of these and other indicators as a way of determining the will of God, we may find some light shed on the question of guidance in general. For it raises a number of problems which go deep into this difficult subject. First, there are essentially practical problems. Why do we seek the will of God–

as something outside of ourselves, and our own general experience of what is right and wrong? It is generally because we suspect our own judgement, we do not place sufficient trust in our own ability to make the right kind of decision. There may be special reasons (I know I would rather *like* to go and live there; the question whether I should take the job must be decided independently). But the general reason is simply that of sin: we are fallen men and women, left to ourselves we will always tend to serve our own interests rather than those of God; and since therefore our own wills are out of line with his, we must find out what to do from him in order to make the right choice.

But what guarantee have we that we shall read the signs aright? How do we know whose voice it is, when we empty our minds in prayer and listen? Is it not possible that it is our own, telling us what we would really like to do after all? That is the real problem, and it is seemingly insoluble. We think it is an advantage to remove making a particular decision from the *normal* processes of decision-making, as if this somehow made it more likely we would make the right choice. Yet this holds true only if we have good reason to believe there to be an objective certainty about the guidance process. There was that kind of objectivity about the God-given Urim-and-Thummim process in ancient Israel. The question is whether we have reason to believe it is there also in our modern equivalents.

And it is difficult to avoid the answer that they are likely to be as reliable, and as unreliable, as the 'normal' decision-making process which they are supposed to supersede (which we may perhaps define as a process in the Christian that is essentially analogous with all human decision-making). Of course it is considered to be fatally flawed by sin. Yet sin is as well able to twist our reading of the promise box or to inject self-serving prejudices into our carefully emptied heads as it is to skew our honest efforts at making a balanced, prayerful and biblically informed decision, in the same kind of manner as we weigh up whether to go to the museum or the park.

To say that is not to trivialise decisions which may have profound implications; it is simply to suggest that there is a fundamental analogy between all human decision-making. Relying on deeply subjective techniques like sticking pins in the Bible and trying to make some sense of the result, or listing coincidences in our experience, will be no more and no less likely to be influenced by my sin than making deliberate personal choices in the context of prayer and in the light of Scripture– but also in the light of day. Indeed, there is reason to think that this may be more reliable, since we are more likely to be conscious of the personal factors and preferences which might influence our choice. We are under no illusion that we have somehow escaped from the need to make our own mind up in the face of what we know about ourselves.

This raises the question of certainty, and there can be no doubt that part of the attraction of seeking God's will in extraordinary ways is that our answers, if that is what they are, have an appearance of objectivity. They seem to be able to by-pass the inbuilt fallibility of our human judgement, of which we are painfully aware in our general decision-making.

But a crucial question to be faced is what kind of status we believe we should attribute to such extraordinary (as opposed to merely ordinary) perceptions of divine guidance. Do we treat them provisionally and therefore humbly ('I may be wrong but this is how things seem to me...'), or do we accord them the status, in effect, of special revelations from God? The problem of whether to regard extraordinary perceptions of divine guidance as essentially analogous with ordinary decision-making (with its mixture of confidence and doubt) or with the reception of special revelation (with its certainty) emerges as the nub of the issue.

It is hard to defend a model of guidance as special revelation, if only because conscientious Christian people are so evidently 'guided' in different directions–on issues like baptism, which are in principle plain alternatives. From a theological perspective there are deep problems of principle with the notion that, through whatever procedure we adopt, we are able to gain direct access to the divine mind. For many people, the use of the kind of extraordinary means of guidance we have outlined is understood to give answers with the certainty of the Urim and the Thummim. Yet this is really a misapprehension, and few would actually argue that, as a general rule, the Urim-and-Thummim analogy would hold.

In fact the test of the status we give to our perceptions of the divine will is whether they continue to be open to review. Do we actively seek further confirmation of the direction in which we are to proceed, once, on the basis of extraordinary means, we have drawn our initial conclusions? In practice this will mean review by means that are ordinary, by the normal decision-making processes; by the means which those who take a different view of guidance themselves normally adopt. Yet if this is the case–if perceptions of the divine will, gained in prayer or from the promise box, are only provisional–then it is hard to see how the claims which are made for them can stand.

But what do we mean by the 'normal' or 'ordinary' means of taking decisions? There is an almost infinite range of possible courses of action which come under this heading. We can only illustrate from the general manner in which human beings use their human judgement. A salesman weighs up the price he can get from a particular customer. An art expert makes up his mind on the authenticity of a painting. The housewife judges just the right proportions of which ingredients will make the best soup. Other, more significant, examples return us to matters which, for a Christian, have a distinctive ethical or religious connection. A young couple ponder whether they should get married. There is a job advertisement in the paper, and the worker who is browned off with his employer wonders whether he should apply.

Now in each of these cases the person concerned will weigh

up all kinds of different factors, and they may include ethical principles operating in the background. In the more serious instances, help may be sought from trusted advisers. But the decision-making processes will all be human, and the human faculty of judgement will be called upon to make the choice. How well the choice will be made must depend on many factors; and, though the judgement of the individual concerned will not be faultless, the decision may prove to be the correct one; or there may be different possibilities, equally good or equally bad.

Christians are called to make responsible human decisions, and it is hard to see how this process can be conceived as anything other than analogous with the general decision-making process in which other human beings are constantly involved. It would be readily agreed that this is the case in certain categories of decision taken by Christians; for example, 'professional' decisions involving acquired skills (such as those faced by the art expert, the salesman and the housewife in our illustrations) do not differ, whether taken by Christians or others. The Christian may seek God's help in facing particularly challenging professional problems. And he or she will regularly lay his day-to-day responsibilities before God. But no special divinely aided process would be claimed or sought in the course of the exercise of those responsibilities.

The question arises in the case of other kinds of decision, in which ethical-religious considerations are present but do not suggest an obvious outcome. This is the middle area outlined above, between those simple ethical questions on which the Bible gives its own guidance, and those issues on which there is general agreement that specific seeking of such guidance is unnecessary: the minor matters which we have already discussed, together with the kinds of decision which we have referred to as 'professional'. There are others which could be added. Granted that there is a considerable area between these two, how is the Christian to discern the will of God?

Rather than seek a special revelation which will give him immediate access to the mind of God, the Christian is called to make his own responsible decisions. We need to recognise that the net effect of the 'extraordinary' approach to Christian decision-making is effectively to by-pass the Christian judgement, and to pass the decision on to God. From one perspective, this is laudable, and speaks of the conscientious desire of the believer to live his life in accord with the divine will. But from another perspective it represents an alternative to responsible decision-making, a passing up of the need to make choices. God is left, as it were, to make the choices himself. Human decision-making has almost come to a halt.

We need to ask whether this is what the New Testament means by obedience, and whether it can really be harmonised with the humanity of the believer. The application of a consistent Urim-and-Thummim view of divine guidance to this entire middle area would be deeply subversive of human dignity. That needs to be borne in mind as more moderate and selective approaches are adopted which nonetheless contain elements of the same principle: let God decide this for himself. And, we must add, there are some alarming parallels between an extreme pin-in-a-text, empty-minded approach and the burgeoning interest in horoscopes and other occult forms of divination; and what they hold chiefly in common is their radical de-humanising of the person.

A Pattern for Christian Decision-Making

What then is an appropriate pattern for Christian decision-making in the light of the will of God? Let us approach the positive question by means of a summary of the chief points of our discussion so far.

First, the Lordship of Jesus Christ extends over the whole of our lives, and we must submit ourselves to him in all things. About this there is no disagreement at all.

Secondly, there is agreement also that there are basic ethical questions on which guidance is plainly to be found in Scripture; and other matters for which it is inappropriate–skills we have acquired and all the minor questions on which we can simply do as we please.

Thirdly, the guidance of God in the Christian life is not some kind of special revelation. We have no Biblical warrant to seek this kind of direction from God, and–given the diversity of 'guidance' which people claim to receive–we have little reason to believe that it actually works like this. There is a major subjective element in our perception of God's will.

Fourthly, our discovery of the will of God is in ways which are fundamentally analogous with the other ways in which we make human decisions. That is, decisions about which we specifically seek divine guidance are not different *in kind* from decisions about which we do not; or from decisions made by people who do not believe in God. They are responsible decisions of the human will, and it is neither possible nor desirable that we should seek to obviate our own human judgement as the source of such choices, enlightened as we would wish it to be by all possible aid. Such aid may take the form of a direct Biblical injunction (Thou shalt not, or Do unto others), or it may include a variety of religious and ethical considerations. If we make our decisions as Christians, then we make them in the unique context of our submission to the Lordship of Christ. But we have still to make human decisions, in all our subjective and sinful frailty.

What then is the unique quality in our Christian decision-making? It is our Christian intuition. 'Intuition' is a good word to use in this context, since it suggests a quality which is human and yet transcends the normal run of human experience. Perhaps the best analogy which we can offer for the Christian intuition is that of the intuition which so frequently develops within a marriage or other close relationship, such that one partner perceives the likely response of the other to some new situation with an accuracy which can be uncanny. Yet it is not telepathy. It is the fruit of a common life in which hearts have been open, desires are known, and no secrets are hidden. Now that is not a perfect analogy, but it says something about intuition and also about the way in which we can take decisions which will please another, and yet which are irreducibly our own.

The focus in our thinking must shift from the passive idea of 'discerning guidance' to the active one of 'making Christian decisions'. The difference in terminology is important. 'Guidance' carries the implication of decisions passed up the line to a commanding officer, and suggests the absence of a decision instead of the making of a right one. The form of prayer as we seek divine help in such circumstances will be decisively affected by our understanding at this point. Do we pray, 'Show me what to decide'? Or do we pray, 'Help me to make a wise decision, as I weigh up the pros and cons'? Our prayer is not for the decision to be made for us; it is for us to be able to make the decision well. The former would detract from our humanity, the latter affirms it and seeks to strengthen it in Christ.

And it raises the question, why have we been given choices? Why *are* there decisions to be taken? The answer lies in the probationary character of our life in this world: we are being trained, prepared, matured. Our humanity is being transformed by the sanctifying power of the Holy Spirit into a humanity fit for fellowship with God in glory. That is why it makes no sense to believe that we should pray, 'What do I do?', when we could pray instead, 'Help me to make the right choice'.

This contrast suggests another illustration, one that is particularly apt. There are many parallels, some of them drawn in Scripture, between God's relationship with us and ours with our children. What is it that we are seeking to do with them, if not to train, prepare and mature them for the adult life that awaits them? So what do we seek from them? Not that they should come to us and ask, 'What do I do here?' whenever a decision has to be made: that is not the way to maturity, but to dependency and the stunting of growth. The question we seek is rather, 'Help me to make the right choice', keeping the decision where it belongs–with them–but opening up the possibility of clarifying the options and their consequences in the light of all that we know of the relationship between us.

Intuition fits well into this picture too. Our children well know what we think about things. They have absorbed our attitudes and made many of them their own, by that informal osmosis which bears striking resemblance to some aspects of the work of the Holy Spirit in us, making us like Christ as he is formed in us and thereby creates in us a new humanity. What we most desire is that they should learn to make their own decisions, and that they should make the best decisions we could wish for them. That is a world apart from the adult son or daughter who seeks parental guidance or approval at every stage, in a bitter caricature of the filial relationship.

As in this example, the fact that God chooses not to make our decisions for us does not imply that he has no interest in our decision-making. Neither does it mean that he has no plans and preferences for us. Far from it. And there can be no doubt that at crucial points in our lives and careers he may have very particular intentions. But the decisions remain ours, and while there will be cases in which he chooses to employ particular intuitions in a striking fashion, we can erect no rule that depends upon, or demands, or even assumes, that this will regularly be the case.

There is a special problem which often arises when guidance is assumed to have been working in an extraordinary manner. The subjective conviction which it brings ('God told me to do this...'), while it can cause some obvious difficulties ('Well, he didn't tell *me*...') has undoubtedly contributed to the divisive spirit which is so often to be found in the evangelical church. For it provides a major discouragement to humility, and a spur to the notion that what I happen to think is also what God thinks: so if you disagree with me, you have set yourself against him. This arises partly from the specific seeking of 'guidance' on controverted issues, and partly because of a habit of mind inevitably encouraged in a Christian life lived around the 'guidance' motif.

Take the example of division in a congregation about some issue on which there are different views. It may be a theological matter like the gifts of the Spirit, or something more practical like what kind of minister they should have, or whether women may take up the collection. If those on both sides of the argument take a high view of guidance–believing that, in effect, there is special revelation available to those who ask in the right way–then both parties will entrench, convinced that the Lord has spoken to them and in their favour. Very reasonably, neither group will yield or agree to a compromise: a great deal of hurt, and perhaps some kind of split, or the departure of leading individuals, can be the result. That kind of scenario has been terribly common in the evangelical church.

By contrast, take a congregation, similarly divided, where another view is held. Contending parties both recognise, in humility, that their view could be wrong. Though they feel strongly, they find peace in compromise. No-one is accused of impiety or lack of prayer. The children agree that they disagree in their intuition of their father's wishes, but agree also that the family must stay together. And there are implications for the degree of conformity which we demand in our fellowships, in matters on which Christians are not of one mind.

We must take care lest a corporate extension of the notion of guidance as special revelation lead us to a view of the church as the arbiter of the will of God. There is surely a lesson in the fact that one of the most controversial of all Roman Catholic ideas, that of the infallibility of the Pope, says little more than that on rare occasions he has the authority to pass on 'guidance' of the special revelation variety. In some evangelical circles there are perilously high doctrines of the authority of the church, and ideas of personal authority which are almost papal in their implications.

Many lesser illustrations could be offered of the way in which the notion of personal special revelation, either in answer to prayer or through circumstance, hardens and divides Christians. It diminishes their sense of perspective, and relegates the humility in which they should learn to disagree to something approaching a vice. The divisions of the evangelical (and broader Christian) world owe much to this single fact. The disparagement and suspicion with which contending parties on a host of theological and practical issues have come to view each other is a disgrace to the name of Christ. It is interesting to speculate on the implications for the Christian world of the simple admission that (in whatever matter divides us) we could indeed *possibly* be wrong; and that, though we think we are right, we do not believe that God has spoken the words 'Yes, you are' straight in our ears.

Which leads us to an even more serious consideration, for this way of understanding the immediacy with which we have access to the mind of God has serious implications for his own dignity. It positively encourages men and women to put words into the very mouth of God. With the best of intentions, the believer who is forever suggesting that 'the Lord led me to do such-and-such, and then he said this to me' is trespassing upon the majesty of the Holy One. When we lose sight of our sinful frailty, and cease to be distrustful even of our firmest intuitions, we have brought God down to the level of the chessboard of our small affairs.

Perhaps most disturbing of all the effects of distorted ideas of guidance is their undermining of reality in the Christian life. Christians who believe that their every decision is dictated to them by God are very seriously mistaken—mistaken in the voice to which they are listening, or in the way in which they interpret their own inclinations. And there will be a tendency for those who do *not* themselves believe that they get this kind of 'guidance' to imagine that they do—or to feel themselves very much inferior. There is a developing pattern of unreality in the way in which decisions are understood by those who make them, and discussed with others and shared with the fellowship at large. The guidance of God, instead of being the experience it is said to be, becomes a convention, and 'spiritual experience' mere talk. We see this same sense of unreality pervading other areas of the Christian life, in marked contrast to the human realism of the Bible.

In that wide range of human life in which Christians face choices–the middle area we have already sought to define–they have no option but to take responsibility for what they decide. They cannot look to God to tell them what to do, with a specially revealed instruction from heaven. But they can look to him, call on him, to aid them in their choice; so the decision they make is an intuition of his will in which their mind and the Holy Spirit resonate with a common purpose, that of parent and child.

Yet it is a human choice, made by analogy with every human choice. It will be affected, perhaps spoiled, by sin. It must remain subjective, and not have more claimed for it than what is true. Yet, carried through in faith, it will conform to the pattern of all God's dealing with his children, and build them up in his image.

CHAPTER FIVE

Emotion and the Heart

Any discussion of the place of emotion in the contemporary evangelical scene is faced with a seeming contradiction. For on the one hand evangelicals are commonly accused of an overly emotional approach to evangelism and worship. And on the other, there is evidence of tendencies which can be described as ascetic or Stoic. They involve the suppression, and imply the denial, of the emotional character of man in the Christian life.

Emotion, Worship and Evangelism

The charge of emotional evangelism is often unfair. The evangelical church encompasses a wide range of practice, here as elsewhere, and it would be surprising if an undue emotional emphasis were entirely lacking. It is certainly less typical than some critics have suggested. Their accusations may depend more on the need to account for the success of evangelism than anything else. Saying that evangelism depends upon emotion is an easy way of disparaging its results.

Of course, it is possible to abuse the emotions, and an experienced preacher (or politician) knows how to do it. But the notion that evangelism, alone of all human activities, should be rigidly divorced from any recognition of the emotional character of man is artificial and unnecessary. Emotion has a due place in every authentically human activity, and the hearing and reception–or rejection–of the Gospel is no more an exception than is Christian worship.

There are all kinds of emotional aspects to our worship of God. They partly fall into different patterns along the lines of the traditions in which we worship. One kind of religious emotion is evoked by silence and ritual, another in the hearing of powerful yet disciplined and reasoned preaching, and another again in the hand-clapping, arm-waving informal devotion which is becoming so common. To point out the profoundly emotional character of each of these traditions is simply to recognise them in their humanity. It says nothing about whether they are good or bad. We each have our own preferences. Unfortunately, partly in order to justify them, we tend to disparage other traditions of worship–often on the ground of their emotional character.

Yet there can be no worship without emotion. The worship of God is the supreme human activity, a foretaste of that eternal homage and fellowship for which man was made. It must involve the whole of the person, and if it does not–if it is, for example, a merely cerebral or formal act–then it simply is not worship, for no man or woman could stand before God in such a pose. So the question is not of the propriety of emotion itself in worship. Indeed, in the book of Revelation we read highly emotional images of our final worship in glory.

What is at issue is the relation of the emotions of the believer to his or her mind. Whether in evangelism or worship, is emotion being used unnaturally? One key to identifying such unnatural and forced use of the emotions would be whether it tended to distort or enhance the truth; to prevent or to aid the working of the human reason. Emotion can certainly be used to short-circuit the normal critical process of the mind. The effect of such a use of the feelings must always be to lessen the personal, and therefore genuinely human, character of the experience. If emotion plays its natural role, it fills out arguments and convictions so as to turn mere words and logic into an experience which is truly personal. Since the Christian faith is irreducibly personal, there is a like abuse in the misuse of emotion or its absence.

A case in point is the question of Christian conversion. The idea of conversion is actually a general one, and people are 'converted' in their politics or their taste in music as well as in their religious faith. There is a particular religious usage in such cases as conversion to a religion such as Judaism or (within the Christian tradition) Roman Catholicism. But the evangelical sense of the term is distinctive. It does not refer to conversion to evangelicalism, but rather to conversion to God.

The idea is widely held in evangelical circles that conversion is either necessarily, or (at least) normally, instantaneous. The common question, 'When were you converted?', implies as much. An answer which suggests that a date cannot be supplied may be treated as prevarication. There can be no doubt that the dominance of this understanding of entry into the Christian life owes much to a largely emotional idea of the experience. If an intense emotional experience is considered to be of the essence of 'being converted', and since intense emotional experiences are concentrated in short spaces of time, the idea of the experience taking three weeks, or three years, is hard to imagine.

Yet there is a real analogy between this kind of conversion and others. The political or intellectual conversion, which can also have a significant emotional dimension, may also take place either instantaneously or over an extended period. And the conversion experience which we commonly call falling in love, and in which the emotional element is at least as strong as in a religious conversion, can equally well be the fruit of a sudden encounter or a steadily developing relationship.

If we ask why evangelicalism has been so powerfully affected by this notion of religious emotion, there are two explanations to hand; one specific, the other more general. Specifically, evangelical thinking has been powerfully affected by the stories of dramatic religious conversion which have been characteristic of revivals and, to a lesser degree, of Christian preaching in general and successful evangelistic campaigns in particular. As we might expect, it is the more dramatic and sudden which have proved the most memorable and, in turn, the most powerful in fashioning the evangelical imagination.

More generally, the stress on emotion should be understood as a reaction against formal and merely notional religion. The history of evangelicalism is in large part the story of such reaction, and formative events like the eighteenth-century revival were above all else the assertion that the Christian religion must be *felt*, that without the engagement of the heart there is no true faith. We touch here once more on the changing sense of identity of the evangelical tradition. For while the alternative is now between evangelical and liberal, before the rise of liberal theology and biblical criticism in the nineteenth century the fundamental cleavage between evangelicals and other Protestants was not strictly theological at all. The alternative was rather evangelical *versus* notional, nominal, formal religion.

This distinctive and, in some degree, anachronistic sense of identity survives in the stress that is laid on the place of emotion in religion. Of course, evangelical Christianity rightly retains its testimony against formalism in religion alongside its apologetic interest in the maintenance of the historic and biblical doctrines of the faith. But the formalism against which the evangelicals of an earlier day protested is a problem which grows less with the decline of the Christian faith as the religion of society at large.

Emotion and the Christian Life

At the same time, it is possible to discern a conflicting tendency at work. For outside the sphere of worship and evangelism it is customary for evangelicals to take a markedly different view of the human emotions. Far from being stressed, they seem to prove something of an embarrassment. To be precise, we find, side by side with an elevation of the place of emotion in certain specifically religious contexts, a tendency to suppress the emotions in typically human areas of experience. It is as if the Christian's emotions had been appropriated entirely for religious purposes, and had no place elsewhere. That is an over-statement, but it shows the direction of this tendency: toward the denial of emotion as a proper part of human experience outside of special religious contexts.

The Victorian poet A.C. Swinburne painted a cruel caricature of the effects of Christianity upon the world. He sought to sum them up in these lines:

> *Thou hast conquered, thou Pale Galilean,*
> *And the world has grown grey with thy breath;*
> *We have tasted of things Lethean,*
> *And drunk of the fulness of death.*

Now, the 'Pale Galilean' is a monstrous parody of the Jesus of the gospels, but it is a parody which aptly draws our attention to the contrast between the real Jesus and the widely-held evangelical ideal of the Christian life. For Jesus was a man with red blood. Nothing is more obvious on a reading of the gospel narratives. Some of the more sensitive and authentic films of his life have brought this out with memorable clarity. And while he was not the creature of his passions, in his self-mastery he made no attempt to circumvent the human emotion which went with incarnation as a man. With the New Testament writers we declare that in his sinless state he was not mastered by his passions. But he was no 'Pale Galilean'.

So why is it that this image of Jesus has become so cherished an ideal of the Christian life? For there can be no doubt that the 'Pale Galilean' has made his conquest in the evangelical imagination. An ideal for Christian living has arisen which owes more to the Stoics of ancient Greece than it does to the Bible. One definition of the Stoic philosophy sums it up as 'control of the passions and indifference to pleasure and pain'. That could equally well stand as a summary of much popular evangelical conviction. It is the doctrine of the stiff upper lip, and it has no place in the church.

For it represents a fundamental denial of the humanity of the believer. It suggests that faith in God renders us immune to the slings and arrows of outrageous fortune. It presents the Christian life as a process of triumph—not simply over sin but over the whole of the human condition. Resting upon the mythical notion that Jesus somehow triumphed in this fashion, the believer is called upon to do the same.

Yet he cannot. Or, at least, if he does, it will be at a price. For the suppression of emotion is achieved, when it is achieved, at the cost of candour and perhaps honesty—and often only by self-deceit. For it is human to be angry and to grieve and to rejoice, and the suggestion that these and other emotions are in themselves sinful or lacking in faith, and that therefore the believer should be able to suppress them in Christ, is entirely spurious—and potentially highly damaging. It is born of over-reaction to the uncontrolled and sinful passions of fallen men and women, and the imbalance it brings to our understanding of the Christian life is as serious as any.

There are many examples of the implications of this kind of thinking in the life of the church. A telling illustration lies in that most trying of all human experiences, bereavement, and—in particular—in the manner in which evangelicals bury their dead. For grief is the human emotion which most pointedly illustrates the two-sided character of Christian living, and at the same time highlights the naïve alternative which has become so common.

As with sin, so with sadness, the key to the authentic Christian approach is never to seek to deny how bad things really are. It is in admitting rather than suppressing the truth that remedy becomes available. Of course, in grief and bereavement this is also a sound pastoral policy; and though that is not our chief concern here, the point is worth noting. The 'keep smiling' principle, common enough outside the church as well as inside, can lead to disaster.

The difference between that and a proper Christian understanding is that it represents an answer which is too easy. It does not comprehend the actual problem, and as a result cannot finally help those who face it–and lead them to rise above their experience. We can picture the alternative approaches in terms of an analogy with sin and forgiveness.

The Christian approach is not to minimise sin, but to maximise the forgiveness that is available for those who repent of it. So if someone has a bad conscience, the natural tendency in the world outside would be to play down the significance of what had been done. By contrast, the Christian will counsel a candid recognition of the fact, not exaggerating its significance but accepting it. There is no need to minimise it, since forgiveness is available. Indeed, forgiveness is not available if the offence is in some way covered up. A full acknowledgement of what has been done is indispensable.

So it is with, in this case, grief. Weeping with those who weep, the Christian will not minimise the tragic character of death. There is no need, for hope is available–hope that does not depend on any naïve, silver-lining reading of the tragedy itself. Indeed, it is part of the key to Christian understanding of tragedy that it does not depend on any such thing. Christian hope, and the comfort of God, are available irrespective of whether we can reach some kind of 'interpretation' of tragic events. Their meaning does not need to lie on the surface and be able to be read by us in order for us to find comfort. What is more, in this way even deeply tragic events can be faced–like the death of little children. For in the place of the 'explanation' which will make sense of what has happened, in place of the felt need of some sort of answer to the question *Why?*, the Christian places his trust in God.

The 'explanation' approach seeks comfort in the lessening

of tragedy, the dulling of the dreadful significance of what has taken place. By contrast, an authentic Christian approach lets the tragedy unfold in all its dreadful character. Instead of struggling grimly to remain afloat, the Christian is content to sink, secure in his confidence that he sinks into the arms of a God who will hold him tight and in his own good time restore him again to the surface.

There are two fundamental problems with common evangelical approaches to death and bereavement. One on which we shall touch at more length in the next chapter is that of the 'explanation' approach to which we have just referred. Evangelicals have a remarkable tendency to fall into the trap of seeking an explanation of events in their experience as a concomitant of their belief in the providential rule of God. That this is not only naïve but unbiblical is something to which we return in our discussion later of man's life in the flesh.

The second problem lies in their tendency to seek to short-circuit the emotional character of grief. Its most obvious effect is to be found in the way in which some funerals are conducted. This is a sensitive subject. Every funeral should not follow the same pattern. Sometimes the acceptance in faith of a loved one's death can lead to an unusual service being entirely appropriate. This may be the fruit of special faith or, as can happen when death has been long expected, it may be the result of a grieving process having begun long before. But there is a tendency for evangelical Christians to believe that the hope of the resurrection somehow short-circuits the tragedy and the grief of death. There is a corresponding tendency for those who do not feel like this to be seen–or, at any rate, to see themselves–as lacking in faith.

There are occasions when it is no doubt appropriate for a funeral service to take the form of a service of thanksgiving. When a Christian dies at a great age, and there are no close relatives or friends to grieve, and there is much in his life or hers for which to give thanks, this is no doubt right.

But on other occasions, it is not. A funeral service is not a time to be happy, it is a time to be sad. The hope of the resurrection does not negate the tragedy; it rather gives confidence that 'underneath are the everlasting arms'. It is a time for the outpouring of our great distress before God, and for us to hear of his comfort. It is not, as it were, for us to come to him having taken comfort already, and tell him how well we are coping.

To put it another way, a funeral service is a place where we go to weep. If we weep, we do not feel we are out of place. If our tears are shed in our heart, we have shed them nonetheless. But if we cannot weep, if we know that the shedding of tears from the eyes or in the heart is somehow improper, then something is wrong. For at Lazarus' tomb, Jesus wept. In the face of death, it was the right thing to do.

And so it is with our lesser sadnesses, and the gravest error of all lies in thinking that because something has happened–whatever it may be–we have some sort of Christian obligation to be pleased. This again we return to in the following chapter. But the simple realisation that as human beings we are actually free to be happy and equally free to be sad, free to make our own human response to whatever turn events happen to have taken–that in itself begins to dignify our emotional responses. It leads us away from the sham and pretence which can so easily result from fatalism and the religious obligation to be pleased with everything. It is a strange irony that those who follow the Man of Sorrows have so often felt themelves, willingly or not, under an obligation to resist sorrow at all costs.

But the key is our freedom to respond to our circumstances. Fatalism seems to imply that the only proper response is one of acceptance, and that therefore emotion suggests an unwillingness to accept the divine will. The effect of this is to lead us to think that not only are human emotional responses sinful, they are unnecessary. The spiritual person will respond with faith and acceptance to whatever life throws at him.

Perhaps the best example is that of anger. There are many

Christians who would consider it simply to be a sin, and for whom the Christian is called to be 'above' such emotional responses to people and situations. In the New Testament we are told not to let the sun go down on anger between Christians (that is, to resolve those things which have given rise to it as speedily as possible), and to 'be angry but sin not', which implies the opposite of the popular view: that anger without sin is not only possible, but something commended to us.

More important, we have the anger of Jesus. It is plain on page after page of the gospels that Jesus is angry with the religious leaders who have misled the common people into a distorted view of God and how he is to be served. This strand in the character of Jesus and his ministry culminates in the famous scourging of the Temple, when we find Jesus using a whip to drive out the money-changers who had set up their businesses in his father's house. He overturns their tables and displays a righteous fury which hardly reminds us of Swinburne's Pale Galilean. Though it may seem dangerous to point it out, it hardly reminds us any more of the evangelical ideal of the Christian life. We say this is dangerous, since our Lord's display of anger had a special significance, and his judgement as to when such behaviour was appropriate was uniquely reliable. But the principle remains: the human Jesus was extremely angry, and did not sin.

In looking at grief and anger we are of course singling out emotional responses to evil and tragedy. What of emotional responses to things that are good and news that is welcome? The widespread evangelical mistrust of emotion is here less obvious, since happiness and joy are distinctly religious emotions as well as simple human ones. Yet if we isolate simple human pleasures that are not also religious in character we discover mistrust here as well. For one thing, the widespread approach to the Christian life discussed in Chapter 3, according to which the only proper Christian activity is that which has specifically religious goals–that approach would in principle rule out human pleasures and other causes of human happiness which were not also in some way 'religious'.

Again, there is an incipient asceticism in many conventional evangelical attitudes. It is partly the fruit of this same idea–ruling out human pleasures on the ground that they are not necessary to the accomplishment of religious purposes. It is partly also the direct result of the mistrust of the emotions: activities which cause human pleasure (aesthetic, sexual, culinary) are suspect as ends in themselves. The lengths to which some biblical interpreters have gone in seeking a reading of the Song of Solomon which can dispense with any notion of romance or sexuality is a striking commentary on this tendency. Whether the romantic and sexual are themselves, in human life, images of something religious and theological is another matter. The point is that emotional pleasure with no immediate religious end or object sits ill at ease in an evangelical view of the world.

We have yet to come to terms with the human-ness of Jesus, which is perhaps more evident in his emotional life than in anything else we are told about him. He is far from being a pale and Stoic figure: on every page of the gospels his heart is pumping with the emotions of sorrow, indignation, anger, joy, surprise, love, grief–the entire range of human emotion, sanctified in his most holy person as in itself without sin. And the implications of this portrait of the Son of God go further, for if we are to be conformed to his image–if we will find ourselves most truly by being found in him–then the 'Pale Galilean' is as much a parody of how we should be as it is of how he was.

Yet it does not only tells us of how he was, it tells us of how he is. The exalted Jesus Christ, in his human nature, is still the compassionate high priest whose heart throbs with love for his people and burns with anger for their enemies. And we should hardly be surprised, that the God who is a consuming fire, whose wrath must be propitiated at so high a cost, whose love has sent his Son to pay it–that this God should, in his own image, make creatures with emotions to reflect his own; or that, in taking human flesh, he should step into the emotional life of humankind and make it his own. So as his Holy Spirit forms Christ within us, we may hope to know more and more of that emotion purged of sin which is ours in our common humanity with him.

CHAPTER SIX

Life in the Flesh

Brother Ass, Francis of Assisi is said to have called his body. The frailty of man is nowhere more inescapable than in his bodily constitution. And it is here that the kinship of Jesus as our elder brother is most striking. For, in him, the Word was made *flesh*; in him all the fulness of the Godhead was pleased to dwell *bodily*. And while both these terms are intended to sum up the whole of the human nature which the Son of God took to himself–the sum, that is, of the last three chapters, as well as of this–it is not only in this symbolic fashion that the bodily, fleshly character of Jesus' existence stands out.

For it is man's physical character that most forcibly speaks of his limitation. What is more, his fleshly embodiment sets him over against the mode of the divine being, which is that of 'spirit'. In incarnation–enfleshment–the God who is spirit took to himself man's own bodily life. God thereby affirmed man's bodily state by making it his own, and affirms it even today since, at the right hand of God the Father Almighty, stands Jesus Christ with his human nature intact in glory.

According to the Bible it was in his bodily form that God constituted man: God breathed into his body and it became a 'living being'. Human life is life lived in the flesh. After death there follows a curious state while those who have died await the resurrection of the dead, when their bodies will be raised up and their constitution as physical creatures restored. Despite the ever-prevalent popular mythology, man's eternal destiny is not to be lived out as a disembodied spirit, but as a re-embodied corporeal creature of flesh and blood. The process of glorification which will fit him to be an inhabitant of heaven will not change that.

Just as the actual denial of Jesus' bodily existence was what constituted full-blown docetism, so it is in the challenges to man's corporeal nature that we find the most fundamental threat to our humanity. A number of different trends in contemporary evangelical Christianity find their–generally unwitting–focus at this point.

The Health of the Body

The question of health and healing has occasioned much controversy, and it is not our intention to re-open it save in a limited degree. The question which has tended to be asked is, Does God heal? That in itself raises the issue of the manner in which healing takes place. What about the miraculous in healing?

Instead, while readily accepting that God heals and that sometimes he heals through miraculous means, we ask the question, Have we a right to expect healing? This is arguably a more important question, for it raises the large issue of God's providential dealings with us as human creatures–an issue to which we turn later in this chapter. What may we *expect* of God?

Well, we may not expect him to deliver us from our corporeal human existence. An obsession with bodily health is curiously secular, and has close parallels in the general attention which the public at large pays to diet, exercise and the prolongation of life. It betrays an absolutising of the body, as if bodily health were an end in itself. To absolutise health and healing is actually to shut out the goal for which, in providence and sometimes in miracle, both health and healing are given.

The notion of healing as a Christian right distinctly carries such an implication. It is akin to (and often believed along with some version of) the notion that the Christian will meet with success in everything to which he puts his hand. This idea has been more common in North America than in Britain, though it is a developed and conscious version of a more widespread and less reflective notion which lies below the surface of much evangelical piety, as we go on to suggest below. It is actually a logical extension of the idea of healing as the Christian's legitimate expectation, since bodily health is only a single aspect of our providential circumstances. If we believe that Christians are singled out for a life in which all will be well, bodily healing needs to be placed in the context of more comprehensive coverage of the human condition and the challenges to our happiness and success.

The 'success' theology in its various forms represents an articulated form of this more comprehensive and consistent thinking. For there is no doubt that bodily health and healing, considered as a Christian right or as in some way essentially obtainable by faith, is inseparable from the other circumstances of human existence in the flesh. The full-blown and crass theology of success has been widely repudiated, but this must not deceive us into thinking that its basic concepts of God, the world and the Christian life are not widely shared, since they are. The hedonistic theory of the Christian life has a natural appeal, despite the evidence of Scripture and experience. And the effect of such a view is serious, since its implication is of a radical denial that the Christian is a true participant in the life of the human race. It has the effect of taking a docetic view not of Jesus, but of us.

Providence and Christian Circumstances

The idea that Christians are supernaturally shielded from the normal course of human events is a common evangelical assumption. Like so many such mistaken ideas, its appeal lies in the fact that it contains truth as well as error. It is true that God's own purposes for his children will be carried through, come what may: in the old saying, a man is immortal until his work is done. The problem is that we do not have access to firm information as to when, in God's own purposes, a particular individual's work *will* have been done. The saying tells us something about God and about the certainty with which he will accomplish his own purposes. It does not, alas, tell us anything about our indispensability in the process. However sure we may feel about the task which lies ahead, we have humbly to admit that the car may crash, or the boat sink, or cancer supervene, and though God's plans will carry on, ours will be brought to a sudden stop.

The idea that Christians are providentially protected from circumstance is consonant with the more distinctive theologies of healing and 'success', though undoubtedly more widespread. It has gained a remarkably broad, though unexamined, influence.

The basic question is this: have we reason to believe that God's providential care for the believer will be such as to ensure that he or she is exempted from the misfortunes which, in a seemingly random fashion, afflict other men and women? The question could be put in another form, and a special case of this general view of providence would depend on some criterion of obedience. That is, if the believer is faithful, then God will provide in a particular fashion for his or her safety/comfort/wealth/health... It is simplest to suggest an answer by asking a rather different question, going as it were from the other end. For the problem of providence and our interpretation of the divine will is extensive. How then are we to understand tragedy and triumph in the life of the Christian?

The Bible in fact provides us with a good deal of guidance on this question, since it is hardly a new one. The answer that has commonly been given is that, since history is in the hand of God—our own personal histories as well as the histories of the nations—then there is a message to be found, written in its pages. And the message is not hidden: it may be read. We can come to some reasonable judgement on the meaning of what has happened. This is particularly true when the history is one of disaster, whether a signal public disaster or the kind of private tragedy which can so terribly afflict our own private world.

It is a natural response, since in the face of disaster there can be few who have not, involuntary, asked–perhaps in great anguish–the question *Why?* The question seems to imply an answer, and an answer is avidly sought, since in so many instances it is believed that it will in some way mitigate the awfulness of what has happened. Bereavement, of course, is the classic case in which this is true: we ask *Why?* in the belief that an answer will actually help. But it is not in this case alone that we ask the question. Disasters, personal and national, are scoured for their possible significance.

One reason for this is undoubtedly the fact that it is at times like this that we feel at our most vulnerable. Our sense of security has been challenged, and our feeling of well-being suddenly exposed to scrutiny. We seek the voice of God with a new desperation, and cup our ears to catch anything we might fancy we hear him saying. We look at the story as if it were a code to be broken, and wrack our brains for clues. What we need to realise is that, though this may be a very natural response, it is simply that. It is not a specifically Christian response. It is the way in which people tend to respond to disaster.

Moreover, as well as being not a specifically Christian response, it is actually not a Christian response at all. It represents a way of thinking about the action of God in history which is repudiated in Scripture. Indeed, it is difficult to think of anything which is more clearly opposed by its teaching. There are two striking examples, one in each testament, in which we meet this very way of understanding history, and find it rejected.

The first is in the Book of Job, or, rather, the first *is* the Book of Job. For the burden of this lengthy narrative is that the kind of pious explanations offered by evangelical Christians to their friends who have suffered tragedy are generally worthless. Job has several friends like that, and their comments are recorded for us at length. They each take slightly different views of the problem, but they have in common the fact that they are wrong. And they are not simply wrong in the particular views they have taken, they are wrong in principle. Job's problems do not have the kind of cause which they suggest. Evidently the Jews of Job's day had much the same idea as people do in ours. It was in error.

Evidently, the Jews of Jesus' day also commonly believed that same thing, for in Luke 13 we find the identical matter under discussion. Some unnamed men come to Jesus with information and a hidden question. They have obviously not paid attention to the lesson of Job. They tell Jesus of the Galileans whose blood Pilate has mingled with their sacrifices–a reference to some violent disorder which has just occurred. Jesus answers them, 'Do you think that these Galileans were worse than other Galileans?', with the implication that he thinks they do. Their assumption is that disaster has come to these men because they in some particular way deserve it. It has avoided the others because they do not.

Jesus goes on to give his own example. A tower has collapsed elsewhere in Jerusalem, and eighteen people have been killed. 'Do you think that they were worse offenders than all the others who dwelt in Jerusalem?', he asks. 'I tell you, No' comes the answer, in the definitive response–from the lips of Jesus himself–to the naïve theory of history as moral cause and effect, believed by Job's friends, and the Jews of Jesus' day, and many evangelicals of our own.

Now to say this is by no means to suggest that history–whether the history of nations, or the histories of you and me–is without meaning. For, of course, the providence of God is what gives meaning to history. And there will come a time when the meaning of history–of every history–will be revealed. The key to the interpretation of our histories will come from the hand of God. That is not in question. The problem is whether we can be in a position to read out the significance of events ahead of that time.

In Scripture, we know, this happens; and the natural tendency on our part to seek to interpret events is certainly encouraged by the fact that in the pages of the Bible we see this being done. What we neglect–in addition to the indications we have noted that the naïve way of reading meaning out of events is simply wrong–is that, in Scripture, the one who can interpret events occupies the office of prophet. Whatever may be our view on whether prophecy is possible today, and–if it is–just what is its character, there is no doubt that those who are not prophets are unable to interpret events; and that the naïve blessing-and-curse scheme of popular imagination is simply wrong.

Which takes us back to our earlier question. If only prophets can interpret the history of nations and of men, and if the naïve notion that disaster betokens judgement and triumph blessing is to be rejected, what conclusion do we draw about the believer's expectation of lifelong providential protection? It would seem to be unwarranted. Not only so. We suggested earlier that it was hard to imagine another issue on which Scripture spoke so conclusively as on this one. The reason is that perhaps the most pervasive theme in the entire corpus of the Bible is represented by the Psalmist's frequent refrain, 'Why do the wicked prosper?' That is, far from reflecting the notion that faithfulness is rewarded by outward blessing, and, correspondingly, disobedience meets with a curse, the position is often reversed. Indeed, there is a *tendency* for the position to be reversed. And in this tendency we see the background to the principle of Isaiah's Suffering Servant, who suffers innocently for the sake of the guilty nation; the principle of the cross, etched deeply on the character of the Old Testament revelation before it is ever made plain in the New.

So what does the believer have reason to expect from the providential hand of God? A consideration of the teaching of Holy Scripture sets man's natural expectations upon their head. The Bible does not teach a theology of success, it teaches rather a theology of failure:

Thrice blest is he to whom is given
The instinct that can tell
That God is on the field when he
Is most invisible...

Then learn to scorn the praise of men
And learn to lose with God,
For Jesus won the world through shame
And beckons thee his road.

F.W.Faber

The entire notion of success, and healing, and protection as
something on which we can rely, something which we as Christians can demand of God, is wholly repugnant to the Bible.
The story of Scripture is one of faith triumphing in the face
of circumstances, and men and women learning to lose with
God.

Of course, there is more to be said. For one thing, there are
particular occasions on which the grace or judgement of God
may bring something about with an obvious significance. A
believer may have a seemingly miraculous escape, from accident or illness. An evil person may meet with tragedy or disaster.
We may well believe that, in a given case, there is a connection
to be made. But we cannot, dare not, generalise; for there are
also believers who are not miraculously, or naturally, saved from
accident or illness. And there are the wicked who continue to
prosper. Special cases we can recognise, but we know of no
general rule.

We must also say that this discussion has focussed on outward circumstances, and that is why it has painted so distress-
ing a picture of what it is to be on God's side in the long conflict
with evil. The man who 'learns to lose with God', precisely
because he has *learned* to lose *with God*, is a man who has learned
the secret of success. It lies not in health or financial reward,
any more than it does in protection from the vicissitudes of life

in this uncertain world. The secret lies in knowing God, and being enabled thereby to meet with both triumph and disaster, and treat these two imposters just the same.

But does this mean that the rule of thumb by which so many Christians have been wont to interpret their circumstances–and, in particular, like Job's comforters, the circumstances of their friends–is fundamentally flawed? The answer must be *Yes*. We have no guarantee of an easy life, indeed we face a likelihood of special difficulties. And if we are tempted to jump to naïve conclusions about others and the work in which they are involved, we must consciously lay aside the inclination to read success as the blessing of God and failure as his curse. There must be other grounds, besides these or in their stead, on which to reach such conclusions.

The prospect for discipleship can be uncertain. Perhaps the most striking of all the Biblical testimony in this regard is to be found in Hebrews,Chapter 11, a passage to which we return in the following chapter for another purpose. It is a catalogue of the heroes of faith, and it chronicles their achievements: Abraham, Moses, David–the great figures of the Biblical narrative, whose lives were instrumental in the working out of God's purposes in the history of his ancient people.

As the chapter moves to a conclusion, the writer asks, 'What more shall I say?' And in the verses which follow he seeks to sum up, not the men of faith, but the acts of faith through which the purposes of God have been accomplished. These heroes 'through faith conquered kingdoms, enforced justice, received promises, stopped the mouths of lions...', and on the list continues. We are reading in dramatic language of just the kind of triumphant acts of faith which we would expect of the people of God. It is a picture of achievement, and glory, in providence and in miracle, as the Spirit of God moves to accomplish his purposes through his faithful servants.

The catalogue continues. They 'quenched raging fire, escaped the edge of the sword, won strength out of weakness, became mighty in war, put foreign armies to flight.' Not only so, and with the sentence which follows we can glimpse the writer's mind moving on to consider a situation in which triumph is at first denied the faithful servant of God, but is finally won by perseverance. 'Women', we read, 'received their dead by resurrection.' But the writer's mind still moves on. For he knows that this is not always so. He knows, as Job knew and Jesus knew, that this is not always how the purposes of God are brought about; that the story does not always have a happy ending.

And even as this powerful chapter comes to its climax, the key changes to the minor. Triumphalism passes into triumph of another order. We move from women who receive their dead by resurrection to women who do not. 'Some were tortured, refusing to accept release, that they might rise again to a better life. Others suffered mocking and scourging, and even chains and imprisonment. They were stoned, they were sawn in two, they were killed with the sword; they went about in skins of sheep and goats, destitute, afflicted, ill-treated–of whom the world was not worthy–wandering over deserts and mountains, and in dens and caves of the earth.' These are they who have lost with God. Their glory is in defeat, their triumph in tragedy, and it is here that we come closest to the heart of the Biblical concept of the providential over-ruling of God in the life and work of the believer.

For not only is there no guarantee of glorious success. There is not even a guarantee of glorious failure. From 'they were sawn in two, they were killed with the sword' we move to those whose very failure is inglorious, and it is these, the unnamed because unknown–not Abraham, not Moses, not David–of whom we read the words of supreme commendation that mark the cadence of this heroic recital: 'of whom the world was not worthy.' It is there, in the deserts and mountains and dens and caves of the earth, that true heroism is to be found.

For Christians are human, flesh and blood, frail creatures

called to live for God but to live also in this world. They bear no passport that offers them safe passage through its dangers, though they know that their course has been charted from above. What they do know is that *God knows* the fate that awaits them, and that therefore the future of failure or success, glory or shame, is in hands that are safe. They are the hands of the God and Father of our Lord Jesus Christ. They led him also along the path of his human pilgrimage, and the way was not smooth. He 'offered up prayers and supplications, with loud cries and tears, to him who was able to save him from death.' 'He learned obedience through what he suffered' (Hebrews 5:7,8). So must we. Whether we may expect to 'escape the edge of the sword' (11:34) or to be 'put to death by the sword' (11:37), we follow in his footsteps, because both alike mark the path of heroism and discipleship which it is our Christian calling to tread.

CHAPTER SEVEN

A Cloud of Witnesses

But what about sin? As we grapple with the concept of a true and renewed humanity in a world in which the only humanity we know is fallen, the Bible offers us two special guides. We have stories of believers recorded in its pages–their struggles with sin and their lives of faith. We have the story of Jesus himself, and his struggle with temptation–to which we turn in the final chapter.

One of the ironies of the evangelical tradition is that, in spite of its polemic against the adoration of the saints, it has developed a 'veneration' of saints of its own. Just as Catholic missionaries are reputed to have replaced local gods with the saints of the church, so evangelicals have replaced those saints with other, evangelical, heroes. They are mostly missionaries, and a sizeable proportion of evangelical publishing is taken up with versions of their lives.

So far so good. The problem is that, as is customary with lives of the saints, these volumes can be misleading. That said, they vary a good deal in quality, and some are useful both as actual biography and also–in the role they are chiefly intended to play–as inspiration. The problem is–and it is the same difficulty which has affected writers of hagiography ('Saints' lives') proper–that when inspiration is the aim, there is a tendency to be less than candid in the presentation of fact.

It need not be conscious, and it need not be the fault of the biographer: good and celebrated Christians are often the victims of flattery and exaggeration, and their shortcomings tend to be eagerly forgotten by those who hold them in high esteem. So the author may find that his materials have already been through a process of selection. He is unlikely deliberately to seek out material of another kind, even if it can be found. He knows that to present unflattering truths in black and white might cause sore offence to the pious men and women for whose benefit he writes. It is in this way that the genre of evangelical hagiography has developed, in which biography does duty as devotional and inspirational reading.

The fact of this development within an evangelicalism determined to be rid of traditional ideas of 'sainthood' no doubt speaks of the need of the human heart for heroes. The same kind of tendencies which led to the cults of the medieval saints have been at work, though under different theological constraints. There is no reason whatever why Christians should not have heroes, and their selection of leading figures from the evangelical past in this role is sensible enough.

The problem lies in the wearing of rose-coloured spectacles, which is dangerous and almost *de rigueur*. While there are some notorious examples of evangelical hagiography, this tendency is in evidence almost everywhere. In a recent and sympathetic review of a respectable biographical study, the reviewer felt himself compelled to point out that the author, in a very extensive discussion, had managed not one line of critical comment.

The practical difficulty with uncritical and unrepresentative accounts of the lives of heroes is that they fail to perform their function. It is a common but surprising misunderstanding of writers and readers alike that what is needed, to inspire the faithful, is a story of the triumphant progress through the Christian life of a plainly remarkable person, whose faults are nowhere in evidence. The whole point of heroes of faith–the function which the saints are supposed to perform–is to give us the inspiration of a half-way house between us, in our pathetic sin and failure, and Jesus Christ, in his sinless perfection. Indeed, the docetic tendency to hold to a mythical and unrealistic idea of his humanity has made it even more necessary for us to have heroes whom we can imagine actually to inhabit the world that we know.

So the tendency of stories of the heroes of faith to become stories of perfection too, putting them on the side of Jesus Christ rather than our side, is entirely self-defeating. They are not half-way houses at all, they are accounts of the lives of those who have triumphed (or so it appears) and led lives of what can only be called effective perfection. In fact, such tales can be uniquely discouraging, since they hold up before us a pattern of Christian achievement which is spurious. No-one ever actually led lives like these, no-one except Jesus. Indeed, there are many aspects to the human life of Jesus, such as his indecision and great anguish in Gethsemane and other aspects of his emotional life, which some Christians would be surprised to find in their heroes.

As we have noted, the mythical, docetic idea of Jesus which has gained such popularity has had the effect of increasing the distance between us and Him–and, in turn, made all the more necessary the development of a second tier of heroes whose humanity has a more realistic quality. Yet the tendency is then to mythologise these Christians just as we have our Lord. The absence of a realistic portrayal, with which we can imaginatively identify and which is actually the key to all effective biography, proves to be destructive of the purpose for which these narratives are written. They resemble less the critical biography of the historian, or the popular biographical *exposé* which the eminent subject tries to get the courts to ban, than the public relations 'biography' whose purpose is simply to adorn the reputation of the one whose name it bears. One of the more disturbing features of hagiography, which distinguishes it markedly from such exercises, is that the subject, usually long dead, would often be the first to object to its saintly portrayal.

Heroes of Faith

The importance of example is underlined in the New Testament, and above all in one place: the letter to the Hebrews. It is written to provide encouragement, and the writer knows that there is no better way to encourage his Christian readers than to refer them to examples of Christian discipleship from whom they can learn. 'Remember your leaders,' he writes, 'those who spoke to you the word of God; consider the outcome of their life, and imitate their faith' (13:7). There is an immediate example in the life and faith of their own church leaders. But there are two other examples which he sets before them, in encouraging the Hebrew Christians to persevere in their Christian discipleship. Consider these examples, he writes; and 'therefore lift your drooping hands and strengthen your weak knees, and make straight paths for your feet' (12:12,13).

The examples he presents are Jesus Christ himself, and the heroes whose faith is set out in Scripture. The Hebrews have to focus upon these two: the Lord himself and those who are marked out in Scripture as having demonstrated signal faith. What is impressive above all else in the manner in which these examples are presented is the way in which the humanity of Jesus, and the humanity of the heroes of faith, is underlined. Unlike the evangelical biographer, and indeed unlike so many evangelical preachers in their presentation of Jesus, the writer of this letter is keenly aware that his readers must be able to identify with the figures he offers them as examples.

We have looked elsewhere at the picture he presents of Jesus in sometimes startlingly human terms; and we return to it in the next chapter. We turn now to the picture of the heroes, in HebrewsChapter 11, the Biblical precursor of the lives of the saints. As we have already noted in our discussion of the later verses, much of what this chapter has to say is lost on many of its readers. We must add to that now, for throbbing through these verses comes a realism that is entirely unsuspected–and, alas, often unnoticed.

For these heroes are plainly partakers with us not simply of human existence but of its fallenness. Heroes they are, but we know them as men and women who, like us, are flawed. We do not know whether the writer of this letter had this in mind when he selected them, though–in the light of his conscious emphasis upon the human-ness of Jesus Christ–the fact that these humans were, as we say, all too human, can hardly have been lost on him.

He did not of course need to select such heroes with special care, for it is in the nature of the Biblical narrative that its heroes are presented to us 'warts and all'. It is deliberately realistic in its presentation of human character. There are few among its major figures free from taint, and that taint is recorded–the kind of taint which would never find its way into a conventional exercise in evangelical biography (except, perhaps, as indicating the life from which the hero was rescued when he was converted). So the sample in Hebrews 11 is a fair sample. It offers us representative Biblical figures as our heroes, and we find them to be men and women like us. They are heroes, they are not supermen.

Who then are these believers of time past? Together they make up the 'cloud of witnesses'–witnesses who watch us and cheer us on, looking down upon us as they stand gathered around the stadium of life; and witnesses also to Jesus Christ, who in their own day were called to bear witness as we are in ours. They are the church triumphant, the host of the redeemed already gathered in glory. Through these representative figures they offer us the encouragement of those who have triumphed already by faith in Jesus Christ. Let us look at some of these figures.

'By faith Abraham' we read (11:8). Abraham is the father of the faithful, the great Biblical example of a man who lays hold on God and whose faith in God is rewarded. But the story of his life, recorded for us at considerable length in Genesis, includes a number of quite disreputable incidents. There is the curious occasion when, apparently out of cowardice, he tries to pass off his wife Sarah as his sister. Most important of all, there is the matter of Hagar and God's promised seed. Sarah despairs of God's promise of a son, and suggests that Abraham have a son by her maid Hagar; and Abraham 'hearkened to the voice of Sarai' (Genesis 16:2). He took Hagar also as a wife, and she conceived and bore Ishmael. This sorry attempt to short-cut the purposes of God was to have grave consequences. Yet, in spite of all this, Abraham remains *the* hero of faith. And we find his wife Sarah getting her own place in the list.

'By faith Sarah herself received power to conceive, even when she was past the age, since she considered him faithful who had promised' (Hebrews 11:11). On any understanding, this is a charitable reading of the Genesis account, yet it could hardly seek to cover over the embarrassment of the truth, since the truth is so well known. In fact it merely draws veiled attention to it. Sarah was eavesdropping when she overheard the Lord himself, *incognito* in a group of angelic visitors, saying to Abraham: 'I will surely return to you in the spring, and Sarah your wife shall have a son.' She laughs, and says (to herself, she thinks), 'After I have grown old, and my husband is old, shall we have pleasure?' But the Lord hears her, and questions her husband: 'Why did Sarah laugh...? Is anything too hard for the LORD?' Sarah compounds her discourtesy and lack of faith by trying to cover up. She lies. 'I did not laugh', she says. But he persists: 'No, but you did laugh.'

Now on any account that is a thoroughly discreditable episode. That it should be taken up and used by the writer of Hebrews 11 *as an example of faith* is remarkable. Yet we read, 'By faith Sarah herself received power to conceive.' There is a kindly judgement on Sarah's faithlessness, and it does not detract from her heroic stature in Israel, even though this incident–like Abraham's faithlessness with Hagar–cuts right to the heart of the significance which the father of the nation and his wife are intended to have.

Moses also figures prominently in the list and, as in the case of Sarah, reference is specifically made to one of the more embarrassing things we know about him. 'By faith', we read, 'he left Egypt, not being afraid of the anger of the king; for he endured as seeing him who is invisible' (Hebrews 11:27). Again, this is a generous judgement. The story in Exodus 2:11 onwards is of his murder of an Egyptian who was beating a Hebrew slave, his hiding of the body, his fear when he realises that 'the thing is known', and Pharoah's determination to kill him. 'But Moses fled from Pharoah, and stayed in the land of Midian.' Of course, we know other things about Moses that would seem to qualify his heroism, not least the final tragedy that prevented him from gaining entrance to the promised land. But the point of this chapter is that, whereas they may have been serious failings, they do not have the effect of diminishing Moses' status as a hero. The life of faith is not a life in which perfection is to be expected, and the realism with which the stories of the Biblical heroes are recorded, while not being uncharitable, enables substandard saints like us to find heroes whose experience of the life of faith does not differ in kind from our own. This is a most important fact.

Then there is Samson, about whom nothing is said here but whose chequered career is candidly recorded in the Old Testament. And, next to him, Jephthah. Jephthah must be the most remarkable of all the inclusions in this list, since his unspeakable act in contorted faithfulness to a foolish vow is one of the darkest stains on the pages of Scripture. Yet he too is there, no doubt selected for this very reason. His dreadful behaviour, which must have stemmed from a deeply mistaken idea of God, does not disqualify him.

David, too, is mentioned. David was the king after God's own heart, whose robust humanity marks him as a man of greatness who had great trust in God. Yet of all these figures it is he with whom sinful men and women can most readily identify. We know that his name is forever blackened by his double act of adultery and murder, and the tragedy which followed. Yet what encouragement there is, that someone like him could survive in the purposes of God; could even be called a hero! What hope it offers, for if God can so regard men and women like that, he might even find room in his plans for someone like me!

The purpose of this rather unusual discussion of Hebrews 11 is in no way to diminish the status of its heroes. Indeed, their inclusion in this chapter guarantees it, since the writer is not working in ignorance of the biographical details which the Old Testament narratives supply. Our purpose is rather to emphasise the actual character of their heroism, since it is the heroism of sinful men and women. Indeed, it is this very point that gives it its significance. It is not the heroism of supermen, it does not rest upon any mythical attribution of perfection to the heroes themselves. They are not commended for their sin, and in particular cases we know that the Old Testament underlines its gravity. It is necessary only to read the harrowing account of David's adultery, its exposure and his repentance to understand the seriousness with which God viewed what he did. The point is that it did not deny his heroism. The extraordinary blindness which led him to act as he did was followed by an equal acceptance of responsibility, and he paid a heavy price.

If we ask the question, 'What kind of men and women were the heroes of Biblical times?', the answer is clear. They were sinners like us; some better, some worse, all alike struggling with sin, but none perfect. Like us they were engaged in a constant struggle with temptation, a daily conflict with sin, and–like us–they sometimes succumbed in small things, or even in great. What characterised them above all was the simple matter of their *faith*. They attempted great things for God, and it was this that made them heroes.

In the light of the candour with which the lives of the Biblical saints are painted, it is surprising how many Christians persist in believing–and desiring to believe–that some kind of freedom from sin attaches to their heroes. Few will admit to believing, in so many words, in sinless perfection. Instead there is an idea which stops short of actual sinlessness, but which still would seem to exclude so many of the Biblical men and women of faith. This, in turn, helps contribute to a lack of candour in our understanding of sin in the Christian life, and a resultant distortion in our understanding of ourselves. We imagine our Christian heroes–in and out of the Bible–as somehow near-sinless, and we try to make sense of our own lives in this distorted image of what it means to live by faith in God.

This results in a twofold effect on our understanding of sin and guilt in the Christian life. First, there is a tendency to believe that, since this near-perfection is demanded of us and we know we do not achieve it, we are failures. Our attempt at the Christian life is a sham. Maybe we aren't really Christians at all. Some such doubt can lurk at the back of our minds and come to the fore in time of crisis, when what we really need is the confidence in God which arises from the knowledge that, sinners though we keep finding ourselves to be, we are living a life of faith. We have to recognise that when the finger is pointed at us, when we *feel* ourselves most to be guilty failures, it need not be the finger of God.

Indeed, if we have sought to do our conscientious best, whatever mess we may feel we have made of our lives, it is most unlikely to be God. We easily forget that there is one whom the Bible calls 'the accuser of the brethren', and there is no-one more pleased when we do forget than he is. The notion that guilty conscience equals God keeping us on our toes is deep-rooted in evangelical piety. And that is just how the devil wants it. One of the hymns has put it well:

When Satan tempts me to despair,
And tells me of the guilt within,
Upward I look and see him there,
Who made an end of all my sin.

For the devil has his own way of dealing with religious people, and it needs constantly to be exposed. We are fed an unrealistic *and unbiblical* notion of the Christian life, and the most pious of us are least able to protect ourselves from the pointing finger of our accuser. We are led by the nose into discouragement in the face of our sin, and matters can only get worse. For if we are discouraged we are more tempted to give up than to call for help. We may give up altogether, having concluded that the Christian life is an impossibility. Or–as often happens–we may begin to retreat from God and the life of the church, maintaining appearances but bothering less and less about our walk with our Lord. It is sadly easy to slide from unneeded feelings of guilt and failure, into discouragement, and then into an increasingly nominal evangelical commitment.

There can be other effects, and one of the most common is a frantic devotion to religious activity. Instead of being discouraged when we feel we have failed, we respond by trying harder, seeking to placate our conscience–and God, as we believe it is he who is speaking to us through it. We never feel we have done enough, and give ourselves to the busy round of involvement in the life of the church–even at considerable cost to our family, or our job. We keep feeling the goads pricking us into further activity. It never occurs to us that this is not the way God treats his children.

There is no place where earth's sorrows
Are more felt than up in heaven:
There is no place where earth's failings
Have such kindly judgement given.

For the love of God is broader
Than the measures of man's mind;
And the heart of the Eternal
Is most wonderfully kind...

Pining souls! come nearer Jesus,
And O come, not doubting thus,
But with faith that trusts more bravely
His huge tenderness for us.

If our love were but more simple,
We should take him at his word;
And our lives would be all sunshine,
In the sweetness of our Lord.

F.W. Faber

There is a second possibility. Instead of responding with guilt, and then either discouragement or zealous activity, the unrealistic portrayal of the lives of the saints and the unrealistic expectations which it carries for our own Christian lives can lead to fantasy. If anything, this is more disturbing still. In short, what happens is this. We imbibe the notion that the Christian life, properly lived, is lived in a state of near-perfection. Since we believe ourselves to be living the Christian life, we conclude that we must not be far from the perfect state.

Of course, put that way it may seem absurd; for that is not how anyone consciously reasons. But the effect of being confronted with a model of the Christian life which is unrealistic and in broad terms perfectionist will be either to arouse the sense of guilt or to dull it. There are some Christians who have been subtly persuaded that the kind of example held out for them in the one-sided biographies is capable of imitation, and–often unconsciously–have modelled themselves on their own particular heroes. They are more likely to be affected in this way if they are temperamentally more inclined toward pride than feelings of guilt. It further dulls their sense of sin, and–along with other factors–helps encourage the particular kind of religious life which we associate with the Pharisees.

We are accustomed to see the Pharisees of Jesus' day as simply representatives of formal religion. What we fail to grasp is that they are more akin to evangelicals whose faith had gone cold than to any other group today. They were the theologically orthodox and zealous group among the Jews. 'Pharisaism' is a particular threat to the evangelical church, and it is fed by unrealistic ideas of the Christian life. It leads to an externalising of sin, into something that is a matter of action (rather than thought or intention) and, generally speaking, something which other people do. The way in which the word 'sin' has come to denote sexual rather than other kinds of sin is one example of this process at work. The central sin of Pharisees in every generation, pride, becomes invisible. The same may be said for lovelessness, ill-temper and much more. A sense of complacency is the result, and it in turn leads to hypocrisy which is unconscious and a formal and external notion of evangelical religion.

The work of sanctification is brought to a halt, and a self-satisfied but conventional religion is the result. It is all a matter of self-deceit. The Christian believes that all is well, for above all else the result of this process is a profound unreality in religious experience.

In both these very diverse processes, of preoccupation with guilt on the one hand and complacency on the other, a failure to grasp the realistic character of the Biblical pattern of Christian living is central. Of course, there are other factors at work as well. Behind them both, the hand of the devil may be discerned, as he skilfully plays on our own particular weaknesses and individual temperament. The man with a tender conscience is made to feel a false guilt. The man whose conscience is robust is tempted to a matter-of-fact approach to his faith which leads to the formal religion of the Pharisees.

What is needed to redress the balance is plain: a realistic pattern for the Christian life. The heroes of Hebrews 11 were great men and women of faith, yet they were sinners still. Their sin was never finally overcome, yet they were constantly engaged in the struggle. Even in the height of their powers and the maturity of their faith, they could fall–and sometimes gravely. Yet they did not find cheap grace: they learned the costly nature of the forgiveness of God. But their weakness did not cut them out of the kingdom, and their heroism by faith led them even to triumph over the sense of guilt and unworthiness which is the natural dress of the faithful man. But, in Christ, he has another, and it is here that his perfection lies: the righteousness of Christ, offered by faith to all who seek it, a sure defence against the lies of the accuser of the brethren.

CHAPTER EIGHT

God's Human Face

We have seen how the humanity of Jesus has emerged as the Cinderella of evangelical theology. As it becomes increasingly necessary to defend the faith, our Christian thinking has become weighed down with the concerns of apologetics. Out of a desire to be faithful to what is commonly being denied, we have grown to stress the divine nature of Jesus and the supernatural elements in his divine-human life in such a way as to imbalance the carefully constructed pattern of the New Testament witness.

We have done this unthinkingly, but the result has been a distorted picture of Jesus in the evangelical imagination. And there lurks a suspicion of any positive interest in his humanity, since so often it has been an alternative to orthodoxy. He has been the subject of misleading and one-sided characterisations, as a social reformer, a revolutionary, or an ethical teacher whose life we are to imitate. Much has been made of the humanity of Jesus because that is as far as interest in him has gone.

This tendency has been exacerbated by the proper emphasis which evangelicals have placed upon Jesus' death, as the prime focus of the New Testament witness. Through an unwitting alliance of these factors–the apologetic stress on the divine and supernatural, and the theological stress on the death–an idea of Jesus has gained wide currency which must be described as docetic, in that it effectively denies his human nature. While they acknowledge the incarnation and therefore the historicity of Jesus, it is hard for many evangelical Christians to grasp with their imagination an idea of this historical, incarnate person as actually flesh of our flesh, and bone of our bone. His human existence in space and time becomes a cipher, a theological necessity in order that there might be a crucifixion.

The neglected but potent doctrine of his continuing, exalted humanity is a particular casualty of this process. Since our notion of the historical Jesus is hazy and even embarrassed, it does not occur to us to begin to wrestle with the idea of this same Jesus after his ascension and glorification on the right hand of God *as still a man*. Yet, as we have already quoted Charles Hodge, 'the supreme ruler of the universe is a perfect man as well as a perfect God' (*Systematic Theology*, vol. 2, p. 637). The pastoral implications of the identity of Jesus in his humiliation and in his exaltation are enormous and largely untapped. As Hodge observes, 'we have all the advantage of His human sympathy and affection; and the form of divine life which we desire from Him comes from Him as God still clothed in our nature' (p. 634).

Apart from anything else, there could be no more impressive statement on the part of God that what we might call the human experiment is not going to be abandoned. We readily imagine that, just as Jesus set his humanity behind him when he ascended to heaven, so shall we; that the human condition has been hopelessly soiled, and that the redemptive work of God in Christ has been directed essentially to rescuing us *out of* that human condition. Yet nothing could be further from the truth, and there could be no more powerful demonstration of God's determination to persevere in the redemption of mankind *as mankind* than his unequivocal and unending identification with us in our flesh and blood. Charles Wesley grasped something of the significance of this fact, and that, together with his interest in the human experience of Jesus, may well help explain the profoundly human quality of the spirituality of his hymns:

Of our flesh and of our bone,
Jesus is our brother now.

We have seen how the writer of the letter to the Hebrews offers in chapter 12 a two-fold challenge and encouragement to his readers. He turns first to the 'cloud of witnesses', the heroes of the church triumphant who 'by faith' have fought the good fight in time past. 'Let us run with perseverance the race that is set before us', he declares, 'surrounded by so great a cloud of witnesses' in as it were the stands of the stadium; and, ahead, 'looking to Jesus the pioneer and perfecter of our faith, who for the joy that was set before him endured the cross, despising the shame, and is seated on the right hand of God' (12:1-3).

This is a dynamic and lively concept, and to speak simply of the 'example' of Jesus is to understate or rather to mis-state his significance. It is here that those who have stressed the ethical character of his teaching and behaviour as somehow isolable from his person—some sort of demonstration enacted for our benefit—have failed. For the example of Jesus is significant only because of who he is. He lived the life of the supremely good man, not as an object-lesson, but as the Son of God, clothed in flesh and blood, doing battle for us with sin and thereby securing for us redemption. We focus our eyes on him, not simply as an ethical example, but as the 'pioneer' of our faith, the one who has gone ahead to secure it for us and in whose footsteps we are to follow. Our imitation of Christ, before anything else, must be an imitation of him in his struggle with sin, his life of faith, and his unswerving commitment to the goal set before him of the joy of the Lord.

It is here, of course, that liberal notions of the imitation of Christ as somehow an alternative to Christianity as a religion of redemption break down. Jesus, as we read of him in the only sources open to us, was no mere ethical teacher and demonstrator. The imitation of the historical Jesus is the imitation of one who set his face to go toward Jerusalem, and who, for the joy that was set before him, despised the shame. There is no other Jesus to imitate. The liberal exemplary Jesus is simply a myth.

And this Jesus is the Jesus of Nazareth, the son of Mary. He who calls us to follow him, and whom the letter to the Hebrews calls our pioneer, was a man. It was as a man that he went ahead of us into the moral and spiritual wastes of human experience, and it was as a man that he came through them. He shared, fully and unreservedly, in our human experience, and the myth which lurks behind all our imaginations and which persists in asserting that he could not *really* have experienced the confines and limitations and uncertainties of human life is simply that: it is a myth. It is conjured of a combination of human refusal to accept the extraordinary depths of divine grace and Satanic denial. For it is the lynch-pin of incarnation and thereby of redemption itself. 'Every spirit which confesses that Jesus Christ has come in the flesh is of God, and every spirit which does not...is not of God' (I John 4:2,3). The human experience of Jesus is no embarrassing excrescence from the main body of evangelical theology, it lies at its heart. And so it is also with *our* humanity.

So it is not without significance that the writer to the Hebrews himself repeatedly underlines the importance of Jesus' human nature. The context is chiefly his concern for Christ's priestly work. For it is here that his representative character as one of us, who has actually lived and experienced our human condition, is central. The significance of Jesus' having 'offered up prayers and supplications, with loud cries and tears, to him who was able to save him from death' (5:7) is *in order that* he might be an effective high priest. The high priest under the sacrificial system of the Jews was chosen from among the people because he had to represent them. It is for this reason that he can 'deal gently with the ignorant and wayward, since he himself is beset with weakness' (5:2). However, like those he represents, he is a sinner; so 'he is bound to offer sacrifice for his own sins as well as for those of the people' (5:3).

The priestly character of Jesus also rests upon his being representative of those on whose behalf he acts. The point in which he differs from the high priest in the Temple is in his being without sin. He still stands on behalf of the people and as one of them, so that 'we have not a high priest who is unable to sympathize with our weaknesses, but one who in every respect has been tempted as we are, yet without sinning' (4:15). The point at which the Jewish high priest is crucially able to identify with those whom he represents is not in his sin, but in his being open to temptation.

So we see here how it is in the experience of temptation that Jesus enters most fully into the human experience. It is in our confrontation with sin that the challenge of discipleship is at its most poignant, for we find ourselves facing a choice between following the 'pioneer' of our faith, and moving in another direction. And we are mistaken if we conceive of temptation as some kind of special, unusual human experience, just as we are if we believe that our Lord's temptations were confined to the period of the wilderness encounter with the devil. Temptation is an unavoidable characteristic of human experience in a fallen world.

So it is that we read, 'because he himself has suffered and been tempted, he is able to help those who are tempted' (2:18): the priestly work is dependent upon a fundamental identity of experience. It is important to understand the lesson of the wilderness temptation narrative, which is the heavy price that Jesus paid in order to resist it at every point. Part of our failure of imagination lies in being unable to understand how there could be a cost involved to the Son of God in resisting temptation. Surely, the argument runs, he could not have given in; and, if he could not, his struggle with the tempter can only have been of nominal significance.

Yet the gospel account of that struggle is unmistakably real, and whatever theoretical understanding we have of Jesus' inability finally to capitulate to the tempter, there can be no room for doubt that the effect of such an inability was the very converse of that which we might at first expect. In terms which Hebrews itself employs, we have 'not yet resisted to the point of shedding blood' (12:4): that is, the entire cross-focussed ministry of Jesus may be seen as one long and determined exercise in the resistance of temptation. The temptations of the wilderness narrative were his life-long companions, as the tempter sought repeatedly–whenever, as the narrative records, he had an opportune moment–to use even Scripture itself to deflect Jesus from the goal which he knew he had been set. The cost to the pioneer was of a different order to that which those who follow have themselves to pay.

At the same time, a nagging doubt remains in our minds as to whether his resistance could have been as costly as ours, let alone more so, since whatever volume of temptation he faced, it was on each occasion impossible for him to embrace it, since his nature was sinless. Yet to believe this is to misunderstand the psychology of temptation, and to confuse temptation and sin. It is no sin to be tempted, and, at the same time, it is impossible to be tempted by that which holds no appeal. If the suggestions of the devil gained a foothold in the consciousness of Jesus, such that temptation actually took place, the mind of our Lord must have been subjectively engaged in sin as a possible course of action.

Now, that possibility was in fact always resisted. We may well believe, with the hindsight of our theological understanding of the incarnation, that such resistance was inevitable. But for our Lord to have been 'tempted *as we are*' involves his grappling with the real possibility of defeat. The question of his consciousness is very difficult, and there are many things we do not know. But we do know that he was really tempted. We have the fact underlined for us, both in the gospels where we read of how it happened, and elsewhere, such as in these passages in Hebrews, where we read why it mattered. And if he was really tempted *as we are* then his experience of resisting temptation must be able to be understood by analogy with ours.

If we approach it in this way, we need first to look at the varieties of our own encounters with the possibility of sin. We could suggest three general categories: sin that we commit unknowing, since our moral sense is not sufficiently developed as to recognise it as sin; sin that–for any of a host of particular reasons–has no appeal to us; and sin which we both recognise and which also has appeal. It is only in this last case that we are concerned with something which we recognise as temptation. And we must re-state its conditions with greater care.

For in saying that we 'recognise' as sin that which we face, we ignore the sophistication in which opportunity for temptation is often presented. There may be a real doubt in our minds as to whether that which we face is actually sinful, and it is in the working through of this uncertainty that our moral sense is proved. The wilderness temptations of Jesus seem to fall into this category, since the tempter addresses him with words of Scripture. The subtlety with which he does so no doubt reflects the greater complexity with which those who are more holy and less susceptible to crasser sins are singled out for the tempter's attention.

Jesus, of course, both discerns the actual moral character of what is being suggested, and repudiates it. He could have done no other. Yet to understand his experience we can perhaps compare it with that of the more holy among us. There are sins that, no doubt, even they commit unknowingly. And there are sins which they recognise to be sins but which have no appeal, and are therefore no temptation. When they face sins which do hold some attraction for them, the struggle may be small, indeed cursory, but it may be great. If they are faced, like Jesus, with temptation which is intense and, at the same time, profound in its implications, they may still resist. Their moral calibre may be such that no other outcome would have been expected, since at the core of their moral being they are compelled to repudiate that which is offered.

But let us be under no illusions: they may pay a very heavy price. A brief example is perhaps helpful. A mature and godly woman, whose marriage has gone sour, falls deeply in love with another man. Let us say that there is no fault on her part. Neither is there any moral possibility, given her character and her convictions, that she will do anything other than draw back from this unsought relationship and repudiate the future which it might offer. But she may pay a heavy price.

For the firmer our moral fibre, the more 'inevitably' we resist even the strongest temptation, the higher the price we may pay. There can be little doubt that Jesus resisted temptation of an order we could not conceive, since if we were faced with it we would crumple, the best of us with the worst. With him, the tempter could keep raising the moral stakes, up and up, until he came to the point where resistance lay only in the shedding of blood.

A telling illustration has been used here. Imagine a rocky shore being battered by ocean breakers. The pebbles which make up the beach are shifted by each wave as it comes in. And there are larger stones, though they too are moved under the pressure of the sea. But there is a great rock, jutting into the air yet founded deep into the shore. The breakers break upon it, but it will not move. It will not, because it cannot. And so it is with the immoveable moral integrity of Jesus Christ. The force with which the breakers seek to shift him is greater than could ever be imagined by the lesser moral creatures whom a big wave will always move. The pressure piles up, but only to be absorbed.

Jesus pays a heavy price as he resists. So, being 'made like his brethren in every respect...because he himself has suffered and been tempted, he is able to help those who are tempted' (2:17,18). The pioneer, the high priest, was one of us, even in temptation. Here, in this most exposed and frail of all human experiences in a fallen world, Jesus took his place beside us, among us, as our brother. And, even as he shouldered the burden of temptation, he shouldered it for us and as one of us. He was no seeming human being, acting a part in human costume. Neither was he a superman, raised above the level of humankind like a pagan god, with superhuman strength to enable him to carry through his moral struggle with corresponding superhuman ease. There was nothing less than, or more than, human about the man Jesus. His human-ness was complete. God himself has become our brother, and shown us what a *man* can do and be.

And this is the crux of the matter, for the repeated tendency of the Christian faith is to seek to evade the implications of humanity. Just as we have sought a mythical model of Jesus Christ whose humanity is a sham, so we have sought a mythical model of the Christian life. The tendency, manifest in so many diverse patterns of Christian thinking today, is to call in question the propriety of being human.

We seek to rise above it. Every facet of our authentic human experience comes under suspicion. We seek to rise above our reason, as if there were some superior way in which we could think about reality. We seek to circumvent our will, as if God's guidance were an alternative to our making informed moral choices (and even choices about matters with no direct moral content); and as if Christians were able–indeed, obliged–to pass on decision-making about matters great and small to God. We shy away from facing up to our feelings, and seek to suppress them in an evangelical Stoicism which is embarrassed by the passions of the human heart. And we struggle even to evade the logic of the corporeal nature in which we have been created, demanding a charmed life as if we could rise above the physical form in which God was pleased to make us.

It is a docetism in reverse, in which rather than deny the incarnation of Jesus Christ, we seek as Christians ourselves to surmount the limitations of body, mind, will and heart with which

God has constituted humankind. Is this, the existence which they comprise, the humanity to which we have been called in Christ, or-in effect-does the Christian life consist in their being displaced?

We may briefly note that behind the assorted, and sometimes conflicting, notions which we have discussed, and which we have suggested add up to a fundamental challenge to our human nature, lie pagan concepts which have surfaced in Christian thinking down the centuries. Most important is the idea of the superiority of spirit to flesh. Largely unrecognised by those who nonetheless hold them, these old ideas have been coined afresh in many of the concepts which lie behind popular Christian thinking.

For example, there is the idea, as unbiblical as it is common, of the 'soul'-understood as an animating spirit which inhabits the body but in fact itself constitutes the human person, the essential self. Then there is the related idea of the life to come as an 'after-life' in which the soul survives while the body departs. These are notions which derive from ancient Greece and have become parasitic on Christian thinking. They foster a lasting suspicion of man as a corporeal being, and undermine our confidence in the Christian life as a human life.

Yet the structure of creation and incarnation tells another story. Man was made in the image of God, and he was made perfect. His humanity, his existence as a bodily creature with will, mind and emotions, far from being evil in fact reflects his constitution as God made him. That is, in the physical and conscious form of *Homo sapiens*-body, mind, will and feelings-man is the image of God, God's finest creature and the one creature made for fellowship with himself.

While we cannot plumb the depths of the concept of the image, we know it means this. Man in his finite and mortal self reflects God. He is as like God as God could make a creature. Nothing less will do justice to the Biblical testimony to the glory of man, and while sin has vitiated and despoiled him, the image remains. The high object of the work of redemption is the restoration of that image in all its brightness, the re-fitting of man to be the companion as well as the creature of God, the renovation of humanity as a form of life which God is not ashamed to call his own.

For in clothing himself in flesh and blood, he has done no less. With an unimaginable grace, he has declared that human life is that form of created existence above every other. As perfect man, and as perfect God, he deigns to rule the universe. And in taking human flesh to himself he finally denies the lure of the tempter that man should seek to become like God.

For what poor Adam could not see was that like God he already was–as like God as ever a creature could be. And though in his vain search to rise above his God-appointed station he succeeded only in bringing down the human race into sin, he could not destroy God's purposes. In incarnation and in atonement his folly has been undone, and God has taken human form in order to lead man back to himself. Adam's folly lay in believing he could ever rise higher than his human station. There is no higher station open to any creature.

That is to say, the purpose of redemption is to enable man to be once more himself, restored to his right mind and his right place as a creature under God. He must put away every temptation to seek something better than his human dignity. The Christian life is the life of man, male and female, made in the image of God and after his likeness. To deny this humanity and attempt to reach beyond to a 'spirituality' which somehow contradicts it, is to fall prey once more to the tempter in his shining, specious livery, who as an angel of light beckons us to reach beyond the confines of our human existence to a place where in fact we deny it and fall from its dignity.

God has become man in order that we might ourselves be men. He has affirmed our human dignity, and far from subverting human life calls us to a spirituality in which what is human is not denied but perfected in him. This upending of so many of the assumptions of conventional piety is strikingly reinforced by the manner in which the life of the Son of God is offered to us in the New Testament. For example, in Paul's letter to the Ephesians his prayer for those to whom he writes is that they may 'know the love of Christ which surpasses knowledge' that they 'may be filled with all the fulness of God' (3:19). That is the high calling of the Christian. And it is a human calling, it does not deny but rather affirms our humanity. The gifts of the Spirit are showered on the church, 'for the work of ministry, for building up the body of Christ, until we all attain to the unity of the faith and of the knowledge of the Son of God' (4:12,13). And in what does that consist?

The apostle is in no doubt. This high goal of the Christian life does not consist in a suppression of the mind, the will, the heart, the body. It is not a denial of man as a created being. It is not an elevation of some spurious 'spirituality' over the human experience of man. It is rather, in the words which come next, 'mature manhood...the measure of the stature of the fulness of Christ'. Mature manhood, measured by the 'stature of the fulness of Christ'. And who is this Christ? He himself is God the Son, exalted on the throne of his universe, but clothed still with humanity. The measure of the stature of the fulness of Christ is the measure of the stature of the fulness of a man.

So it is that in our response to human*ism* we must never deny what is human. The humanist affirms the humanity of man, and as he does, so he does well. His failure is not in what he affirms, it is in what he denies. And as we respond to him, as we call in question the adequacy of his understanding, it is his reduction of human nature to the merely human that we reject. We do not seek to escape the human, for there is nowhere we can go. There is no super-humanity, and every step in that direction is in fact a step toward the sub-human; not a rising, but a falling. Adam sought to rise above his humanity, and since there was nowhere he could go, he fell.

The failure of the humanist lies not in his indulgence of the humanity of man, corporeal, intellectual, volitional, emotional. It lies in his failure to grasp that these marks of man, taken as ends in themselves, are the very marks of sin. Under God, they mark the true character of the man who bears the image of his Maker. The superhuman Jesus, far from being accorded a higher dignity, is no human Jesus at all, a mere seeming man, a sham of God incarnate. The superhuman man–the man whose 'spirituality' has denied his humanity in his effort to be like God–is a mere subhuman, a mere seeming man, a sham of the image of God. Like Adam, there is nowhere up that we can go. We can only go down.

There is therefore absolutely nothing to be ashamed about in being a 'mere' human being, since there is nothing 'mere' about human nature. To be human is to be made in the image of God, and there is nothing higher to which we can aspire. For to be made in the image of God is to be made as much like God as someone who is not God could ever be. This amazing dignity, which attaches to human nature wherever it is found, is finally proved to us in Jesus Christ, since in the incarnation God took to himself the mode of existence which is also ours. And having once taken it to himself, he has not laid it down. Then and today and for all eternity, human existence is dignified by the astonishing fact that the God who created it has made it his own.

And the human nature which the Son of God took to himself, once and for all, in Mary's womb, is not super-human. He is no superman, and the critical importance of this fact is underlined by the decisive rejection of docetism by the early church. He is no superman, since there is no such thing as 'superhumanity'. Any supposed advance on humanity is really no improvement at all, it is rather a deterioration. You cannot become super-human, only sub-human. Every attempt to go one step up simply takes us one step back. Nothing is higher than the image of God. How could it be?

THE PLIGHT OF MAN AND THE POWER OF GOD

Dr Martin Lloyd-Jones

The text of the highly esteemed sermons given by Dr Martin Lloyd-Jones, based on verses from Romans, Chapter One, focuses on our need to be entirely committed to the Christian gospel.

Dr Lloyd-Jones highlights the uniqueness of the faith. Because of this he stresses the necessity of our absolute commitment to Christ and his call to us.

This book will be of great interest to all thoughtful Christians and of help to preachers, speakers and students.

THE NATURAL TOUCH

Kim Swithinbank

Some people think of 'evangelism' as knocking on doors, reading your Bible on the train or starting up conversations with strangers in which you get on to the four-point-plan-of salvation as quickly as possible. Some of these activities we would do, others we'd cringe at doing.

In his first book, Kim Swithinbank says that sharing our hope in Christ is something that we are *all* asked to do. It should be as natural as breathing to us.

Taking us through the most common obstacles which keep people away from Christianity, he shows how we can develop a lifestyle which is attractive and compelling for Christ.

Kim Swithinbank is Director of Evangelism at All Souls, Langham Place.